# ECHOES I
# RIPON'S I

CW00471108

Over 100 illustrated articles on the
history of Ripon

Editor

*Mike Younge*
Ripon Local Studies Research Centre

Copyright:
Mike Younge
Ripon Local Studies Research Centre

ISBN
0-9547077-0-2

Published by
Ripon Local Studies Research Centre

2004

Designed and printed by
The Max Design & Print co,
York, England

*Mike Younge died suddenly on 9th February 2004. At the time of his death he had completed the writing of this book, and was in the final stages of preparing the copy for printing.*

*It is the profound wish of his wife and daughters and of the Research Centre that this book be published as a fitting memorial to a well-respected man.*

# Contents

CLARENCE HOUSE

I was delighted to be asked to write the foreword to this collection of articles on the history of Ripon - a charming, unspoilt city with ancient traditions for which I have the greatest affection. For a number of years now, I have been helping to promote its regeneration which I would like to think was initiated by the ideas put forward by my Institute of Architecture at the time of my visit to Ripon in 1994.

It is encouraging how much of that regeneration has been completed, allowing more attention to be given to Ripon's greatest asset, its historic past, which in so many ways reflects the history of the country as a whole.

I would like to congratulate Ripon Local Studies Research Centre for producing this admirable publication which deals with so many aspects of Ripon's past and deepens our understanding of this remarkable cathedral city, and I would commend it both to the people of Ripon and to those who visit it.

# Preface

The opening of Ripon Local Studies Research Centre in October 1999 at No. 42 Market Place focused new attention on Ripon's past, since research into the history of the ancient city is one of the Centre's declared aims. Almost immediately it began to publish in the *Ripon Gazette* a series of weekly articles touching on aspects of Ripon's past, and this continued for the next two years.

The eventual publication of the 100th article was seen as the right moment to close this series, but encouraging comments from readers suggested that it would be worthwhile reproducing the articles in book form, especially for the benefit of those who complained that they had forgotten to keep some! The decision to go ahead with the book project was taken when it was learned, through the good offices of Mr. Michael Abrahams, that Prince Charles would be pleased to write a Foreword to it.

Ripon Local Studies Research Centre is very grateful to the Prince for this honour and would also like to tender warm thanks to all those whose names appear on the list of Sponsors, since without them the necessary funding would not have been available.

In deciding the format of the book it was thought appropriate to retain the individual identity and journalistic style of the original articles as well as their occasional cross references. The text however has been updated and slightly expanded with new illustrations added, and the number of articles increased to 103.

Mike Younge
Editor
February 2004

# Sponsors

Mr. Michael D. Abrahams, C.B.E., D.L.
Miss Connie E. Birkinshaw
Mr. Craig Bennett (The *Black Bull*)
Mr. David Bowen
Mrs. Jane Compton
Mr. Ian and Lady Deirdre Curteis
The Chapter of Ripon Cathedral
Miss Jean Denton
The Freemasons Ripon Chapter
The Getty Trust
Mrs. Margaret Hare (The *Royal Oak*)
Harrogate Borough Council (District Councillors' Fund)
Mr. John R. Hebden
Mr. Michael Hutchinson
Messrs. Lishman Sidwell Campbell & Price
Mr. David M. McFarlane, B.D.S.
F. E. Metcalfe & Co.
Sir Ken Morrison
Mr. Christopher & Mrs. Rosalind Norris
Ms. A. Maureen Pratt
Professional Indexing Services
Ripon City Council
The *Ripon Gazette*
Ripon Historical Society
Ripon Local Studies Research Centre
Royal Engineers Association
Mrs. Maureen Small (The *Unicorn Hotel*)
Staveley Historical Society
Mr. Martin Sterne
Mr. John P. Sylvester
Mr. Richard Taylor
Mr. Colin & Mrs. Margaret Waite
Mr. Toby & Ms. Annabel Wallis
Wolseley Centers Ltd.
Mrs. Carole Younge

# Acknowledgments

Ripon Local Studies Research Centre would like to thank the many people and organisations who have provided information and illustrations to help bring this book to fruition.

Whilst we have made every effort to trace the copyright of illustrations, this has been especially difficult in the circumstances and we extend our apologies to anyone whose permission has not been formally obtained.

# Snippets from Medieval Ripon - Part I

## A hard-headed cleric

Roger de Ripun was very fortunate. A cleric at York Minster, he was taking part in Matins one day in the 13thC when a hefty slab of stone fell from a height in the Norman choir and hit him on the head. Amazingly, far from being killed, he was not even injured, and this was immediately deemed a miracle wrought by York's local saint, St. William.

The stone was given an inscription and added to St. William's shrine, whilst the whole incident was later depicted in a stained glass window. When such shrines were broken up at the Reformation the stone was thrown out, only to be rediscovered and rescued in 1867. It is now on display in the Minster Undercroft, and the medieval inscription stating that the stone fell 'SUPER CAPUT ROGERI DE RIPUN' can still be clearly read. Obviously men of Ripon in those days were made of strong stuff.

## Will ye no come back again?

Following the English disaster at Bannockburn in 1314, northern England was much troubled by Scottish raiders bent on seizing wealth and doing maximum damage. In May 1318 a marauding host, having burnt Northallerton, reached as far south as Ripon, which was looted whilst the people took refuge in the great church for three days. A deal was struck; the people handed over six hostages (volunteers?) and promised to pay 1000 marks (£650) if the Scots left without burning the town.

A few days later the Archbishop ordered the collection of the ransom money, but........ two years later the money had still not been paid and the six hostages were still in Scottish hands. A rare document survives - a petition from the wives of the hostages asking King Edward II to compel Ripon to hand over the ransom due, so they could get their men back. Unfortunately the final outcome is not known, but it is likely that with the danger past, the appeal fell on stony ground.

### Rival supporters create a fracas

Celebrating the feast of St Wilfrid with a four day fair sounds a great idea, but it could also bring trouble, as it did in 1441. Order was supposedly kept at the event by the heavily armed soldiers of the Archbishop of York, but as they also guarded the toll collectors and tended to take the place over, their image was somewhat tarnished.

Moreover, there was a rival force in town - the Knaresborough Foresters, always ready to prove their worth, and whatever taunts were exchanged in the Market Place, the showdown came later at Helperby when the Archbishop's men were ambushed on their return journey to York. In the ensuing fracas many were seriously injured, including the unfortunate Christopher Bee, who "had his cheek-bone broken and his teeth knocked down his throat so that he could never eat or speak properly afterward".

## Snippets from Medieval Ripon - Part II

### Doing penance

Those convicted of acts of violence in medieval times could choose to be punished by the church, in which case an act of penance was imposed after which they received absolution. The act of penance imposed in 1452 by the Ripon Chapter on some men of violence required them to walk in procession to the church, with bare heads and feet, each man holding a burning candle and his sword (held point downwards). These were then deposited at the shrine of St. Wilfrid as an offering to the saint. In another incident a year later a similar penance was imposed except that the malefactors had to wear only a sheet and walk in procession to the shrine on six Sundays. All this may have caused embarrassment, but the church's mild punishments were naturally preferred to being flogged or mutilated!

### Treating animal disease by branding

In addition to the offerings of pilgrims, the Minster Church in medieval times enjoyed an income from the local livestock farmers by letting them hire out a remarkable device called St.Wilfrid's Burning Iron.

Diseases of sheep and cattle were treated by applying the heated iron to their backs, much like the branding of steers in the American West, and no doubt the ceremony was accompanied by a few carefully chosen words uttered on behalf of St Wilfrid. Hiring out the Iron brought in a tidy income in the 15thC, as records reveal (29 shillings 9 pence in 1419) and in 1520 takings soared to 107 shillings - but it was not to last. Superstitious practices such as this lost favour with the coming of the Reformation, and in the 1540s were abolished by Parliament, leaving the Chapter to count their pennies ever more carefully.

## Trial by squeezing

Ripon has always needed its tourist attractions and in medieval times the greatest attraction was undoubtedly the shrine of St Wilfrid which attracted pilgrims from many miles away. A problem arose when saints' shrines were closed down and broken up in the mid-16thC. Visitor numbers no doubt fell dramatically and in time new attractions had to be found.

With great economy of effort, the answer found in Ripon was to convert the saint's relic chamber to a new use - a supposed chastity test for women. One of the candle niches in the wall was knocked through into a passage way to produce a narrow aperture through which a slim girl might squeeze, and so prove her honour. No doubt many failed and regretted having tried, whilst onlookers enjoyed their discomfort.

The attraction came to be called St. Wilfrid's Needle, and was as special to Ripon as the Hornblower. Not long ago visitors to the crypt could still see how the sides of the Needle's eye had come over the years to be worn smooth with the struggle to succeed. The custom continued sporadically until after the Second World War, so there are surely some Ripon 'Needlewomen' still alive. A Grand Reunion sometime perhaps?

# The Charter Horn and Baldric

### How old is 'old'?

Ripon's most treasured civic possession has to be the Charter Horn, hung from a badge-studded baldric proudly worn by the Sergeant-at-Mace on ceremonial occasions. Enclosed in velvet and bound with silver bands, the Charter Horn has long been the symbol of Ripon - but there are still several unanswered questions about it.

How old is it? It is certainly older than the 1604 Charter and therefore goes back to the time of the Wakemen. A description of the Horn survives in the Wakeman's minutes of 1603, which mentions its black velvet cover, its silver tips, bands, chain and 'escutcheons'. The earliest surviving escutcheon is that of the Wakeman of 1515, and clearly even then the Horn and Baldric were held in high regard; they were also both carved in stone in the north nave aisle of the Cathedral at about this time. So how ancient is the Charter Horn?

Although 'King Alfred's charter of 886' is now well known to be mythical, there is a serious possibility that the Horn does date back to late Saxon times when horns were used as presentation pieces to symbolise the granting of lands or rights, and served as hard proof that such a grant had been made. Such a horn is the Horn of Ulf in York Minster which later had similar silver mounts added to it and is thought to commemorate the grant of the former lands of the Viking lord Ulf to the church c.1030 by King Canute. But if Ripon's horn commemorated a grant of about that date, its nature still remains a mystery, as does the origin of the post of Wakeman, with whom the Horn was so closely linked. (The age issue could be resolved by the carbon-14 dating of a tiny sliver of the horn).

Later adorned with emblems of the trade guilds as well as a silver spur and crossbow, the fortunes of the Charter Horn and Baldric have fluctuated over the years. Revered in 1603, it survived the Civil War successfully but then fell a victim to the pride and carelessness of a Mayor, Christopher Hunton (1686/7), who put the civic treasures out on display in his inn, the *White Hart* (now Morrison's), and then found that many of the silver adornments had disappeared. He was fined for his negligence, but it was over a decade before the losses were made good - by a later Mayor, the public spirited John Aislabie (1702/3).

Since the 17thC the Baldric has been periodically restored and embellished by the addition of many more Mayors' badges, there now being so many that a second baldric has come into use. In 1986, however, exactly 300 years after the Hunton debacle, the Horn was lucky to survive an even greater threat when valuable items of civic plate were stolen from the Town Hall.

The embodiment of Ripon's historic past, the Horn in accordance with ancient custom is still carried in public procession before the Mayor on five 'Horn Days' through the year, including of course Mayor-Making day.

## The Wakeman

### Keeping watch over the city

The previous article on the Charter Horn made reference to the Wakeman, Ripon's unique chief office-holder in medieval times. What other town ever had a Wakeman in charge of its affairs?

Mayors began in Ripon with the 1604 Charter, but the origins of the previous post of Wakeman are lost in the mists of time; it may even date back to late Saxon times, but there was no Market Place in those days. Reliable details of the annually elected Wakemen only survive from the 15thC, but by the end of the 16thC we have a clear picture of their role and duties. The reason for this is that in 1598 the all-powerful Archbishop of York was asked to sort out problems in Ripon's town government, and he did so by issuing *The Towne Book of Rippon* in which the revised rules are set out.

This rare and valuable document makes it clear that the Wakeman's main purpose was to preserve law and order, and with the help of constables and servants he kept a special night watch from the horn-blowing at 9 in the evening until dawn, looking for 'evil and unruly persons'. As he had plenty of day jobs too, one wonders when he ever slept! If break-ins and robberies took place during the Watch, the Wakeman had to pay compensation to the victims, but the people in turn had to pay for this service – 2d. for one door and 4d. for two - and could be fined if their houses were not properly secured. The Wakeman also enjoyed an income from the 'Market Sweepings', the corn dues later collected for the Mayors.

His other duties included arranging a supper for the Aldermen after a torch-lit procession, holding an end-of-year dinner for the Aldermen and their wives, and officiating at their funerals. The Wakeman was not to be trifled with - those who spoke 'scornful, opprobrious or slanderous' words about him could spend a day and a night in the stocks. Because of his many duties (including ringing the Fire Bell and protecting the Town Bull), the Wakeman was forbidden to "flitt out of the town or sojourn elsewhere" during his year of office - unless plague had broken out.

It would seem that he was also there to uphold moral standards, and had the power to fine those who "harboured whores, whoremongers and common strumpets". We learn that in 1567, John Birkbie, "suspected to be a notable fornicator.....hath diverse times in the night time bene taken abroad in the towne of Rippon by the Wakeman and other officers with lewde women". His fate is not recorded, but it turned out that he was the rector of "Moremonkton"!

Easily the best known of the Wakemen was the last one, Hugh Ripley, who began his year of office as Wakeman and finished it as Mayor (1604). He deserves credit for his efforts and expenditure to secure a Charter of Incorporation for Ripon, which established the Corporation and officers that the town retained in modified form until 1974. Mayor three times in all, he died in 1637 aged 84, and his restored monument can still be seen in the Cathedral.


# The Hornblower

## Staying in tune with the times

No one needs to be reminded that the Horn symbolises Ripon and that the nightly horn-blowing ceremony on the Square is one of Ripon's 'ancient charms'. The Hornblower's job is an important one - he needs both dignity and humour to

The Ripon Hornblower.
"The Horn is blown every evening at 9 o'clock, opposite the Town Hall."

impress and entertain the large crowd that frequently gathers around him on summer evenings.

Like the Wakeman, the post of Hornblower can be traced back without difficulty to the last years of Queen Elizabeth I. *The Towne Book* of 1598 states that the horn was to be blown every night at nine o'clock at the four corners of the Cross, and despite the lack of reliable clocks in those days, this practice was clearly followed. The horn-blowing marked the setting of the watch, when Ripon's chief citizen, the Wakeman, took on personal responsibility for keeping order during the night with the help of his constables, and any victims of burglary and theft could claim compensation.

Even in 1598 the horn-blowing custom was well established and it is probably as old as the Market Place itself (12thC), the creation of which would make law and order there a matter of public concern (as it has been ever since). By the early 19thC it had become the custom for the horn also to be blown nightly outside the Mayor's house, and the lamp (1892) which designated his residence was re-sited each year until 2002 when it was given a permanent home over the door of the Town Hall. A replica lamp now goes the annual rounds.

Over the years a number of horns have come and gone (like the one used in 1598); the 1690 horn is now safely in retirement, the one in use today dating from 1865. Little is known about individual Hornblowers before the 19thC but in early Victorian times the post was held by the exceptional Benjamin Simmonds of whom it was said that he exceeded all his predecessors in the length and strength of his blast. He held the post for 30 years until his death in 1846 at the age of 82, but his son John Simmonds, who succeeded him, showed even greater stamina, holding the office for 41 years. He died in 1887 aged 85, perhaps exhausted by his exertions during the great Millenary Festival the previous year.

The Hornblower was paid for his work, and his wages naturally increased over the years, if somewhat erratically. Despite already having had a pay-rise in 1831, in 1836 Benjamin Simmonds' remuneration was raised from 30 shillings a year to 52 shillings - a 73% rise. And in 1961 the Hornblower's wages were dramatically increased from £52 a year to £200!

A plaque giving details of the Hornblowers from the Simmonds' time onwards can be seen on the north face of the Obelisk, generously provided in the 1980s by the then Deputy Hornblower Joel Bastow, the only American so far to hold the post.

The Annual Convention of European Night and Tower Watchmen is to be held in Ripon in 2004, and Horn-blower equivalents from many other countries will meet in the City to enjoy themselves and no doubt compare costumes and performance - a very special event by any standard.

# The Bellman

### Opening the market and giving out the news

To those who frequent Ripon market on Thursdays, the Bellringer is a very familiar figure, as dressed in his formal uniform he proclaims the market open at 11.00 am with a resounding series of 'dongs' from his handbell.

Like the Hornblower, the Bellman's office is an ancient one, and may well date back to the time of the Wakeman - there was certainly a Bellman by 1668 when the Corporation had to pay for his new coat cloth. Other recurrent costs over the years included his badge, his staff, his tricorn hat and of course his bell (nine shillings in 1677).

In past centuries the Mayor was entitled to a toll, the 'Market Sweepings', levied on corn set out for sale, and trading could only begin when this tax had been collected - the go-ahead being given by the ringing of the 'Corn' bell. The toll was discontinued in 1849.

What were the Bellman's other duties? It is clear from the photograph that he also served as the Town Crier, an office which has unfortunately died out. In 1673 when there was an important announcement to be made, the Corporation had the news proclaimed in the Market Place and also "did order the bellman to tinckle the bell throughout the towne".

As is the case today, the Bellman would walk in civic

processions, but in Georgian times he also appears to have been responsible (and could claim expenses) for cleaning the Market Place, posting up notices, lighting fires for Corporation meetings, and acting as their courier (1802: "ordered that the Bellman's fees for making calls in the town in future be threepence each, and fourpence for the country").

One of the duties which a vindictive Bellman would have enjoyed was chastising malefactors in the Square on market day, using a cat o' nine tails, an event which would certainly have contributed to town centre entertainment. In 1800 George Wills, Bellman, was "paid 5 shillings for each whipping".

The identity of several Bellmen is known, one of the earliest (1749) being William Bell who presumably got the job on the strength of his name. Mention must also be made of John Gregg, Bellman for nearly 30 years (1853-82). We are told that "having a powerful and well modulated voice, his fame soon spread abroad and many matches were made as to which town had the best bellman". Apparently he was also very athletic, and "backed himself to leap any toll-gate in the neighbourhood, a feat which he accomplished on several occasions". Even this man's health eventually gave out, and in 1882 he was succeeded firstly by his son-in-law James Flinn, a tailor from Coltsgate Hill, and then in 1886 by his grandson Anthony Flinn.

The Bellman's role as Town Crier can only have lapsed in comparatively recent times, as this Edwardian picture makes clear; Town Criers are great fun for tourists - is it perhaps time to re-instate the custom?


# The Obelisk

### Designed by an architect and an inspiration to artists

This etching is a copy of the fascinating painting of the Market Square produced by Julius Caesar Ibbetson, who after much travelling spent the last twelve years of his life working in the Masham area. He loved market place scenes and this picture bears all the hallmarks of his style. It would date to the period 1805-17. His widow Bella, who was 35 when he died, rather remarkably then found employment at Studley Royal as housekeeper to Elizabeth Sophia Lawrence, and soon married again, this time to John Britain of Ripon, a grocer turned banker and property dealer. Britain, already himself widowed, owned the Market Place property opposite the Wakeman's House now occupied by Stead and Simpson. He was Mayor of Ripon three times, and on the last occasion, 1831/2, Bella was Mayoress. The Market Place as she would have seen it in that year would have changed little from the view depicted here by her first husband some years before.

If the Regency date is correct, then this is the earliest known picture of Ripon Market Place, and it is therefore very important. There are many points of interest - the cobbled surface, the horse transport, the staggered roof lines, the Georgian bow windows, and the entrance to Fishergate not yet widened, leaving the building which now houses Thomas the Baker four bays wide, not two.

But perhaps what catches the eye most is the Obelisk with the four mini-versions around it. The original obelisk was of course built by the enterprising and imaginative John Aislabie in 1702 during his year as Mayor of Ripon. Aislabie brought in Nicholas Hawksmoor to design it and persuaded the great and the good of his day to stump up half the cost (he paid the rest). The Archbishop of York gave £50, the Dean and Chapter rather less. The plinth was to be "set rough...to keep idle persons from making letters and writing what they please upon it, and doing other Mischieves and Brutalities".

However, whether the problem was vandalism or stone erosion, the obelisk was in need of repair by 1735, and more urgent attention in 1781, the work this time authorised by John's son William Aislabie in the year of his death - as an act of filial piety? A later account of 1798 states that the "obelisk, being in a ruinous condition, was taken down and a new one erected, superior to the former, at the sole expense of the late William Aislabie, Esquire". By 1785 a grateful Corporation had added the commemorative plaque which we see today.

Around the Obelisk in the picture can be seen the four mini-obelisks which figure in other illustrations of the early 19thC. Presumably the 'fenders' listed in the accounts of 1702, they were to survive for many years, finally being removed in June 1882. Do they still lurk somewhere in the city?

Seven years later, in May 1889, the obelisk underwent another renovation, though less radical than William Aislabie's. The stonework was re-pointed and a protective oil coating added. The copper horn at the top was re-gilded and the opportunity taken to convert it into a time capsule by including within it the current minutes of the Highways, Finance and Sanitary committees. In 1985, when the obelisk was again renovated, these proved a rather less exciting find than the hoped-for Aislabie gold coins, but recent research has at least demonstrated that the Obelisk is the oldest freestanding monumental obelisk in England. It still forms the focal point of the Market Place and serves as an ideal backdrop for the nightly horn-blowing ceremony. Its Tercentenary was duly celebrated in 2002.

# The Late Victorian Market Place

## When a Russian cannon was a war trophy

What immediately catches the eye in this winter scene is the cannon enclosed in railings at the foot of the obelisk and pointing at the Town Hall! This Russian cannon, captured at Sebastopol, was set up in the Square in April 1858, in a public expression of triumphalism, two years after the close of the Crimean War. After twelve rounds had been fired up on Red Bank the trophy was drawn to the Square by the Yorkshire Hussars and set in position before the eyes of the City Corporation in their robes, and several thousand spectators.

In the years to follow, however, the cannon seems to have acquired a nuisance value, as it took up valuable market space, and finally in 1896 the Corporation decided to re-site it on a stone base (which still survives) at the east end of Kirkgate. Its ultimate fate was to go for scrap metal to serve another war effort. History was to repeat itself in 1916 when a captured German gun was paraded through the city.

To the right of the obelisk stands an elegant drinking fountain erected in December 1873 as a personal memorial to a Susannah Paterson and piously inscribed "May it lead all to seek that fountain of living water where thirst is unknown". Despite its practical value the drinking fountain too lost favour and it too was removed in 1896 to a site near the court house. Its final resting place is unknown.

Whilst this undated photograph is therefore earlier than 1896, it is later than 1882, since three of the six gas lamps can be seen which were installed in that year around the Square, and the mini-obelisks removed.

Details of the shops are interesting, even if a magnifying glass is required! The main feature of interest is no doubt the block of properties which separated Queen Street from Middle Street in those days. At the south end, facing onto the Square, was Robert Aslin's hosiery and lace business which by 1897 would become John Rayner's draper's shop. It was threatened when the Corporation began the widening of Queen Street in 1902; as described in a later article a dispute over compensation delayed its demolition until 1905, by which time it stood alone in splendid isolation.

To the left can be seen Ebdell's shop, also a draper's but gone by 1897. Further to the left was Fletcher's highly regarded confectionery business which flourished in the 1890s but it too was soon to go (by 1901). Adjacent to it was G.R. Raper's City Boot and Shoe Establishment, in a building originally four bays wide, later reduced to three as seen in the picture, and then in 1902 to two bays when Fishergate was again widened.

Finally, on the west side of the Square, can be seen the twin gables of Nos. 23 and 24, the further of which, the *George and Dragon* pub, had already long been there and was to survive until 1986.

Soon after this picture was taken, and certainly by the time of Queen Victoria's death in 1901, major changes took place on the Square; apart from the removal of the cannon and the drinking fountain, a dozen lime trees were planted around the perimeter, concrete was laid over the cobbles, and the underground toilets arrived on the scene - changes of a similar magnitude to those of 2000/2001.

# Ripon Fairs

## Problems in the Market Place

Fairs of one sort or another have been taking place in Ripon for centuries. Then as now they continued over several days, but in the early Middle Ages they coincided with major church festivals.

The lucrative right to hold a fair was granted by the Crown to prominent local dignitaries, and in Ripon's case that meant the Archbishop of York. The grant was made by King Henry I in the early 12thC, and the fair was a four-day affair centred on the Feast of St. Wilfrid. Until the Market Place was laid out much later that century, it is likely that the fairs were held around the great church, as was common practice elsewhere. Medieval fairs were dominated by the sale of livestock, but other merchandise would be on offer too, and there were no doubt minstrels and diverse forms of street entertainment for the benefit of pilgrims and fair-goers.

The Archbishop's officers regulated the fair and collected the various tolls involved. This was not a popular task and could lead to violence, as in 1441 when the toll-collectors with their armed guards, on their return journey to York, clashed with the Foresters of Knaresborough who had been at the fair (see article 1). After the 16thC Reformation, control of fairs passed increasingly to the town authorities.

More detailed information survives from later times, revealing that by then there were specialist fairs at different times of the year. By the late 17thC, Ripon like Boroughbridge was famous for its horse fairs, held in what is now North Street. 19thC trade directories reveal a rota of fairs running throughout the year, mostly for horses, sheep and cattle, but also including a wool fair in the Old Market Place in June. The November cattle fair, accompanied by the inevitable fairground entertainment, was also the time of the Martinmas Hirings, when servants and farm labourers could be hired for the coming year.

By Edwardian times the full Fun Fair had arrived, especially around Wilfra-tide in early August, bringing with it swings, roundabouts, boxing booths, steam organs, etc. - far too noisy for some visitors at the *Unicorn* in 1906, who cut their stay short and left. Another problem stemmed from the livestock, which often obstructed the roadway and fouled the cobbled surface of the Square, leading to it being concreted over in 1900 and the eventual transfer of livestock sales to the Auction Mart in North Road.

Although the Thursday market continues unabated, the traditional fairs gradually lapsed in the early 20thC, as selling animals and making whoopee found separate locations.

# The Market - Part I

## The eager huckster and the careful housewife

As previously noted, the Archbishop of York's fairs in Ripon lasting several days were authorised by Royal Charter in the early 12thC, but in 1292 there is also specific reference to a well-established Thursday market. Like the fairs, the weekly market was controlled by the Church, and there was money to be made from them, particularly of course from stall charges. As always, townsfolk needed the produce of the countryside, and for centuries the market was much concerned with the sale of corn, meat, poultry, butter, eggs, fruit and vegetables. A market hall was discussed but never built.

Interesting observations on Ripon's market were made by Celia Fiennes, a much travelled lady who in 1697 noted on a visit to the town "we were there the market day, where provisions are very plentiful and cheap. In the market was sold then two shoulders of veal - they were not very fat nor so large as our meat in London, but good meat, one for 5d., the other for 6d., and a good quarter of lamb for 9d. or 10d., and it is usual to buy a very good shoulder of veal for 9d. and a quarter of beef for 4s.; indeed it is not large ox beef but good middling beasts; and craw fish 2d. a dozen - so we bought them".

Despite church control the Corporation too imposed its dues - if only on the Corn Market (held opposite the *Unicorn*), where 'Market Sweepings' were levied, originally a handful of corn out of every sack for sale. The Bellringer at 11 o'clock authorised corn dealings only when that levy had been collected. This ancient right was finally given up in 1849 but the traditional Cornbell is still rung. The Corporation was also responsible for checking the weights and measures used by

13

the traders - in 1732 the miller Christopher Pinckney was prosecuted for selling a bushel of corn below weight.

In the 19thC there were significant changes in the control of the market which was now slipping from church hands. Although in 1837 the Archbishop transferred the tolls to the new Bishop of Ripon, twenty years later they were handed on again to the Ecclesiastical Commissioners (1857) who used the Corporation as their agents - and then in 1880 Ripon Corporation itself bought out the market tolls for £1500.

Ripon's weekly market in late Victorian times was described in the following terms at the time of the great Millenary Festival of 1886: "The scene is one of busy activity. Heavily laden carts and waggons bring in the country produce, which is readily purchased by the eager huckster or the careful housewife....... Surrounding the venerable obelisk.....the vendors of butter, eggs, and poultry assemble to dispose of their commodities.......The loud ringing of the bell by the city Bellman announces that the Cornmarket is now open, and thither farmer and merchant wend their way to transact business on the local exchange. Fruit and vegetables, implements of husbandry, hardware, dry goods and other commodities may be found in their respective quarters of the market; and from all these the city toll collector levies the usual dues".

## The Market - Part II

**Responding to market forces**

Perhaps the most significant change in the character of the Market over the last hundred years has been the growing diversification of goods for sale. Where once it dealt in farm produce which people bought for the week to come, for many years now it has offered a wide range of manufactured goods alongside the traditional fish, fruit and vegetables.

This had become evident even in Edwardian times. In 1906 farmers attending the Corn Market complained about the "vendors of pills, pots, parrots, canaries and other articles crowding the Market and plying their trade with such vehemence that the legitimate business of corn sales could not be properly carried out". But times were changing. In 1921 an attempt by the Corporation to increase the stall charges only for those selling manufactured goods was opposed by indignant traders in drapery goods from Knaresborough and Leeds, who forced a compromise settlement.

If the Corn Market was in decline, so too was the cattle market, although the re-surfacing of the Square in concrete in 1900 was done largely to help keep it clean in the future. Controlling the animals was another matter - in 1913 a young heifer broke loose and barged into a draper's shop, no doubt to the great consternation of the customers inside.

The picture shows a rather small market in 1927, yet market tolls fell from £781 in 1928 to £569 in 1931. The Great Depression was blamed, but so too was

the development of motor transport and other supposed factors. The Market has no doubt had many ups and downs over the centuries, but it survived the problems of the Thirties too, and was then faced with the austerity years of the Second World War.

The latter half of the 20thC saw other changes: the transfer of control in 1974 from Ripon Council to Harrogate Borough Council; the replacement of wooden stalls by sturdier if less traditional metal stalls; the introduction of a Saturday fruit and vegetable market and more recently the occasional Farmers' Sunday Market (plus Craft Stalls). Some traders like Carricks continue to support the market as they have done for over 50 years, whilst new traders are joining the scene from as far away as Oldham.

Over the centuries the market has shown great resilience in adjusting to changing needs and is as popular as ever, as any fair weather Thursday will bear witness. 2001 brought major improvements to the Square, including its repaving, and Ripon's ancient Market is now housed in as fine a setting as any in the north of England.

## Cabs, Charabancs and Omnibuses

### Being taken for a ride

Public transport in towns has changed dramatically over the last hundred years, but in Victorian times the horse was king. The well-off had their private carriages whilst poorer folk either walked or paid to use public vehicles. The latter could mean horse-drawn trams in the big cities; in Ripon it meant either hiring a cab or catching the omnibus.

Market Place omnibuses took on an essential role after the opening of the railway station in 1849, running a shuttle service to meet the trains. For many years the main provider of these coaches was Thomas R. Mountain whose office was in Fishergate, behind which lay the great workshop of the Royal Standard Carriage Manufactory (more recently Greenwood's and part of Woolworth's). But from the 1850s an omnibus service was also based on the *Unicorn* hotel, and for the rest of Victoria's reign these two services had right of entry to the North Eastern Railway Station Yard on Ure Bank. In 1904 Mountain's omnibuses were withdrawn, leaving the *Unicorn* as the sole provider of the railway connection.

Horse-drawn cabs (cabriolets) for hire were introduced from France in the early 19thC and various styles developed. The famous Hansom cab (two wheels, with driver at the rear) does not seem to have caught on in Ripon, where a more stable 4-wheeled vehicle was favoured, as the picture shows. Well before 1900 the cabmen had established their rank down the east side of the Square, across the road from where it is today but not, it would seem, on Thursdays when the stalls took over that space.

By Edwardian times motor vehicles were growing in popularity, and the *Unicorn* omnibuses adapted accordingly. The cabs followed suit, but if the cabmen had to learn new skills, their need for greater comforts during the waiting periods led to a very welcome development - the provision of a heated shelter where they could also read, chat and snack. The Corporation had accepted the need to provide such a shelter as early as 1904, but it did not actually arrive on the scene until 1911, and then only through a generous bequest from Miss Sarah Carter, the daughter of a former Mayor. Newspapers and magazines were to be provided.

The Cabmen's Shelter remained a distinctive feature of the Market Place for many years, but by the early 1980s it was little used and had much deteriorated. It could easily have gone for scrap, but was saved by the intervention of Councillor Rowley Simpson, himself a taxi-driver, and was later acquired by Ripon Civic Society. The Society had it painstakingly restored and then handed it over to the City Council; it has since made a welcome return to the refurbished Square and is now part of its traditional street furniture.

Control of the taxis, their numbers and their maximum charges has rested with Harrogate Borough Council since local government reorganisation in 1974.

## The Post Office

### Regularly on the move

In this early Edwardian view of Market Place South, the gas lamps (1882), the trees (1897), and the underground toilets (1899) have all been commented on in previous articles. In the distance is the *Unicorn* Hotel, with Etherington's Drapers & Costumiers next door where the Skipton Building Society now stands - the entrance to Kirkgate had yet to be widened.

The Town Hall (1800) is little changed, but the buildings on its west side were then occupied by Christopher Lickley's hairdressing business and by Ripon's Post Office - where the Halifax Bank now is. This was however by no means the Post Office's original location in the town.

Although Ripon townsfolk had apparently been requesting a Post Office since Queen Anne's reign, the first officially recognised Post Master of whom details survive was William Farrer a century later - bookseller, banker, historian,

magistrate and twice Mayor of Ripon. In the 1820s his Post Office was on the north side of the Square where Thomas the Baker is today. Letters could be collected there or left for despatch to York (6d), Leeds (7d) or London itself (11d).

A surviving poster of 1847 in the *Unicorn* hotel records that by then the Royal Mail Coach left Ripon at 6.45 every morning. Its days however were severely numbered - within two years Ripon was on the railway network. The trains were making the postal service much faster, and Rowland Hill's Penny Post (1840) was also making it much cheaper.

By 1832 the Post Master was Thomas Proctor, also a printer and bookseller, working from Farrer's former shop. He resigned in 1857 after falsifying his stamp accounts, but his daughter Elizabeth was allowed to succeed him, although she soon (1859) moved the Post Office to new premises in Kirkgate (next to the Duck Hill railings). There she ran the business with the help of her two younger sisters and four 'Postboys', two of whom in 1861 were aged 60 and 68! She eventually retired as Postmistress in 1891.

About then however the Post Office migrated back to the Market Place, to take up the premises shown in the photograph. At the time of the annual Martinmas Fair in 1897 the Postmaster complained that cattle and sheep standing in the roadway were obstructing the entrance to his Post Office! The picture is pre-1906 for in that year the Post Office moved yet again - this time to a purpose-built location in North Street (now Monty's Night Club). The then Postmaster was William Watts.

Even that however was not to prove the final answer: fifty years later, in 1956, there was yet another move, this time to its present premises in Finkle Street (formerly the Mechanics Institute), although the Sorting Office continued in North Street for some years.

# The Town Hall

## The High Society meeting place in Regency times

The grandest building around the Square is undoubtedly the Town Hall, now just over 200 years old. However, given the considerable width of its street frontage, it is no surprise to discover that, like the National Westminster Bank, the Town Hall occupies a site that once contained two adjacent properties, each with its own story.

The westernmost building was an inn in the late 17thC, though its name has not survived. In the 1690s the proprietor was Ellen Horner, a widow, who also owned the *Unicorn*, and the Corporation rented one of her parlours for their meetings, but they were slow payers, owing her eleven years rent (£11) in 1688! In the early 18thC the inn passed to the Chambers family, and then in 1723 to the Aislabies of Studley Royal. Meanwhile, the property next door on the east side had also been held by the Horner family in the 17thC before it too was acquired by Studley Royal, this time in 1766.

Following William Aislabie's death in 1781, the Studley possessions were inherited by Elizabeth Allanson, his married daughter, whose fine painting still looks down on all events held in the Council Chamber. A lady with architectural taste, she decided that her two properties on the south side of the Square should be demolished and replaced by Assembly Rooms. Ripon Corporation would however still be allowed to hold their meetings there (after being temporarily re-located to the *Unicorn*).

Work began in 1799. The architect James Wyatt designed the building with five bays and a pediment supported on half-engaged Ionic columns. In front there were iron railings. The best room, reached by a fine staircase, was the Grand Salon (now the Council Chamber) where local notables in Regency times would gather for balls and official dinners, having bought their numbered season tickets.

On Elizabeth Allanson's death in 1808, ownership of the Assembly Rooms passed to her niece, Elizabeth Sophia Lawrence, but in the 1830s, when political reform took place and several Whigs councillors were elected, the Tory owner of the building in a fit of annoyance banned the Corporation from meeting there. It was not to return until 1851, by which time the Earl de Grey controlled the Studley estates.

In the late 19thC the building took on more of the character of a modern Town Hall. There were visible changes to the exterior too - in 1859 a gas-lit clock was

*Ripon . Assembly*
*1st Subscription Ticket*
*22nd September 1801*

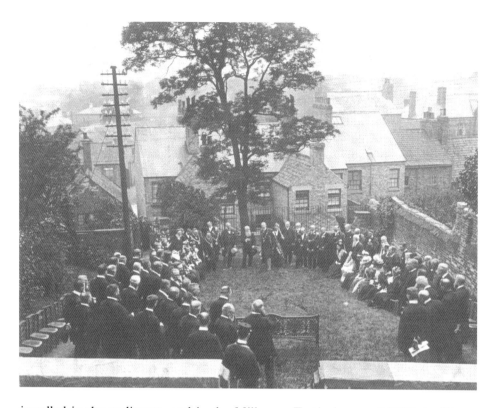

installed in the pediment, and in the Millenary Festival year of 1886 the Ripon motto *"Except ye Lord keep the Citie ye Wakeman waketh in vain"* was added beneath it. Relations between the building's owner and the City Corporation were now greatly improved, and when the Marquess of Ripon became Mayor in 1896, he marked his year of office by formally presenting the Town Hall to the City (1897). Funds too were raised to present the Marchioness with the elaborate and expensive Mayoress's chain which has since been one of Ripon's finest civic treasures.

In 1974 ownership of the building changed again, as the new Harrogate Borough Council took over, but the Mayor and City Council have retained rights there, and use the Town Hall to receive visitors, among them the Queen, and more recently, Prince Charles.

## Hugh Ripley's House

### We seek it here, we seek it there

The imposing Georgian upper storeys of what is now the Halifax Bank remind us that this building has a long history. At the close of Queen Victoria's reign it served as Ripon's Post Office, and there are still people who can remember when it flourished as the Lawrence Restaurant and Ballroom before and after the Second

World War, a popular centre of local night life, but earlier buildings on this site have had prominent associations with Ripon's history over the centuries.

Out of sight below ground is stone ashlar walling from a high status medieval (?) structure, fortunately recorded when opportunity afforded some years ago. In the early 17thC Ripon's most famous old-boy, Hugh Ripley, last Wakeman and first Mayor (1604) lived here in what would have been a black-and-white timber-framed house not unlike the nearby building wrongly attributed to him today.

From Hugh Ripley the house passed via his daughter to the Holmes family and later to

IN RIPON
IT IS, OF COURSE
"THE LAWRENCE"
RESTAURANT · CAFE · BALLROOM

THE LARGEST AND BEST APPOINTED CATERING
ESTABLISHMENT IN THE CITY

Our Kitchens have just been re-built and re-equipped with the
most modern appliances

OUR TWO AIMS—QUALITY AND SERVICE

R.A.C.

Phone : Ripon 47          Managing Director : Cecil J. Gay

William Chambers, an apothecary and thrice Mayor of Ripon, who died in 1714, aged 60. The property was then inherited by his son, also a William Chambers, also an apothecary (and surgeon), and also Mayor of Ripon (1741/2).

The story now takes an unusual turn. A little earlier, about 1730, this Dr. William Chambers received into his household a young distant relative (b.1723), inevitably also called William Chambers, who attended the Grammar School and lived in Ripon through the 1730s. It was almost certainly during these years that his guardian had the house rebuilt in brick, creating the superstructure which we still see today - one of the Market Place's best Georgian facades.

Perhaps witnessing these works as a boy inspired the younger William with an interest in architecture? After leaving Ripon in 1739 he travelled to India and China with the Swedish East India Company and then underwent a formal architectural education in France and Italy. In 1757 he was appointed architectural tutor to the Prince of Wales, and later, with Robert Adam, Architect to the King (George III) and Comptroller of the King's Works (1769). Knighted in 1770 and a Fellow of the Royal Academy, Sir William Chambers designed Somerset House in London and the Pagoda at Kew Gardens. He is reputed to have designed the Coronation Coach still in use today. He died in 1796 and was buried in Westminster Abbey.

His one-time guardian had died in 1753, but the Chambers family memorial can still be seen in the floor of the Cathedral, in the north nave aisle near the crossing.

Indisputably, this is a house with a history.

# Hugh Ripley: Last Wakeman, First Mayor

## A veteran campaigner for Ripon

As Ripon's most famous personality from the past, Hugh Ripley comes second only to St. Wilfrid himself. The Hall in Skellbank commemorates his name, and there have already been a number of references to him in these articles. As is well known, his claim to fame stems from the fact that he was both the last Wakeman and first Mayor of Ripon at the time that King James's Charter (1604) introduced this change, but closer inspection reveals that his personal story is full of interest and merits a study in its own right.

He was born about 1553, when the Ripley family were already well established in Ripon, and became a mercer, dealing in expensive textile fabrics. He was clearly a successful business man, acquiring properties and land in and around the town, and in 1604 was chosen as Ripon's Wakeman. The previous year King James I had succeeded Elizabeth on the throne, and Hugh Ripley was keen to secure a formal royal Charter of Incorporation for the town from the new monarch.

It was later recognised that he deserved much credit for securing it, but seven years later he was still owed money by the Corporation for personal expenses incurred at the time. Appropriately enough, when the 1604 Charter was put into effect (it can still be seen in the Council Chamber), Hugh Ripley became the first Mayor. His year of office must have gone well, since he was asked to serve as Mayor twice more, in 1616-7 and 1630-1. Always generous with his own money, it would seem, he was owed 30 shillings by the Corporation in 1609 for providing

wine for the Archbishop of York during a recent visit. That same year, Hugh Ripley, now an Alderman, was authorised by the Corporation to experiment with the making of *'teill'* on Ripon Common and to go ahead "if it be found for the good of this whole Corporation". What mystery substance was this?

In April 1617 James I visited Ripon, and Hugh Ripley must have been disappointed to have ended his second term as Mayor only two months earlier. He was however given the job of arranging for a pair of spurs and a gilt bowl to be presented to the King, later deemed to have been "a contentment to his Majesty".

Hugh Ripley lived to be 84 and made his will only in the year of his death (1637). He had much property to dispose of and bequests to make. As is perhaps now well known, he never did live in the 'Wakeman's

House'; his house (with two servants) being further to the east where the Halifax Bank now stands. The house was to go to his grandson, but Hugh Ripley's widow Mary was to occupy a special extension at the rear (a granny-flat?).

Interestingly his will also made provision for land rents to provide extra income for the Mayor (no doubt reflecting his own personal experience). Other rents were to go to 40 poor people of Ripon yearly for ever, and also as loans to help five poor tradesmen and to pay for a poor child's apprenticeship. To his brother Thomas he left his best gown, his doublet, jerkin and breeches. His only debt was £7 owed to his wine merchant!

# The Wakeman's House

## Once neglected, now highly valued

The flags which are part of the exuberant decoration of the Wakeman's House in this photograph may suggest a national occasion, but the plaque above the word *Precious*, the surname of the family of basket-makers who had occupied the premises for many years, tells another story.

The photograph was taken in July 1904 when Ripon was celebrating the Tercentenary of the grant of its Charter by James I. Instead of being simply part of a manor of the Archbishop of York, with its leading citizen the Wakeman having primarily policing duties to perform, Ripon was changed by this charter into an incorporated Borough with the power to make its own bye-laws and to hold its own court, and its leading citizen was granted the dignity of the title of Mayor.

The credit for this increased independence has been given to Hugh Ripley, 'last Wakeman and first Mayor', so it is hardly surprising that this house on the corner of the Market Place which local tradition held to have been Hugh Ripley's home,

was so much a part of the celebrations in 1904, celebrations which included the usual Cathedral service, the laying of the foundation stone of the Spa Baths, together with many more light-hearted attractions and ending with a firework display.

The connection of this house with Hugh Ripley stems from an oral tradition which is un-supported by any other evidence, unless reported appearances of Ripley's ghost at the window can be claimed to be such! Unfortunately the documentary evidence points in a different direction for the location of Hugh Ripley's home - to the rather less picturesque property now occupied by the Halifax Bank next to the Town Hall.

But whether one believes the tradition or not, it is certain that it has contributed to the house being preserved to remind us of what Ripon used to be like; however, the belief once held that the house was medieval has given way to modern opinion that its basic structure is no earlier than the sixteenth century, though archaeologists have found medieval pottery on site.

The tradition is not the only reason for the preservation of the building - another is the two and a half centuries of 'benign neglect' by the owners, Cravens and Rockliffes, who could not easily sell it because of a family settlement, and had little incentive to rebuild or modernise it as for most of the 19thC they lived elsewhere (at Asenby and Nunwick).

Neglect and tradition then had combined to produce a situation where changes in the law having at last made it possible for the owner to sell, enthusiastic members of Ripon's Corporation could persuade those reluctant to saddle the Corporation with such a dilapidated building to purchase the property in 1917 - from Sidney Moss, grocer, who had bought the house two years earlier in order to secure it. In the early 1920s it was extensively restored by Alderman William Hemsworth to whom we owe much of its present facade - but it still remains the most intact early timber-framed building in Ripon.

Since the 1920s the problem has always been how to provide funds for its maintenance. As a result the building has had a variety of different uses - warehouse, antique dealer's shop, café, tourist information office, craft shop (some of these in conjunction with a museum at the rear). Since 1974 the property of Harrogate Borough Council, and again restored in 2002, it hopefully now has a guaranteed future ahead of it.

# Thirlway's

### Now you see it, now you don't

These photographs often cause surprise to those who have long assumed that the small paved area at the top of High Skellgate has been an open space for centuries. In fact the demolition of the Thirlway property there took place as recently as 1946, and was done to improve the road junction.

The photographs were probably taken about 1900 when the shop was known as Thirlway & Son, Stationers and Booksellers. Thirlway's business occupied the site for over 120 years and locals called it Thirlway's Corner. The family moved there as tenants in 1815 from Middle Street (now part of Queen Street) and eventually bought the property in 1832.

The previous owner had been John Britain, grocer, banker, property developer and three times Mayor of Ripon. In 1829 Britain had purchased it from the Governors of the Grammar School who had earlier leased it to various individuals in the 17thC and 18thC including Jeffrey Adamson, the calligrapher who won fame by making a copy of the 1604 Charter for the Corporation in 1608. Britain rebuilt the property, squeezing it somewhat in the process as the pictures show - the first improvement to the junction.

Henry Thirlway, the founder of the printing, bookbinding, bookselling and stationery business was a thrifty man, always on the look out for a bargain, but not mean. He played an active part in church life and in local politics on the Tory side. He loved company and music, and was physically active, enjoying long walks. At the age of 69 he surprised the company at a

Ball in the Town Hall by leading the country dancing with the wife of a local draper.

When his only son Henry Steel Thirlway (b.1820) was about to be married in 1850, his father handed over the business to him. Despite being an intensely serious-minded young man he shared many of his father's characteristics, including a love of music, walking and dancing. In his youth he spent time with his father at the seaside and on business/holiday trips to London. He too played an active part in the church and in the Mechanics' Institute. It is due to Henry Steel Thirlway that we know so much about his family and times, as for a number of times he kept a detailed diary which was published only a few years ago. Of particular interest is

his description of the building of the railway which was to link Ripon to Leeds and Thirsk - Thirlway enjoyed frequent walks along the track as it was being laid. In the photograph he can be seen, aged about 80, standing in the doorway of the shop.

His son, Henry Mann Thirlway (b.1851), the last of the family to run the business, like his father and grandfather was a well known local character. In his youth he became known as a first class shot, but his chief claim to local recognition lay in his long service on the Council. Both his father and grandfather had served briefly on the Corporation but Henry Mann Thirlway was a member for over 40 years and was twice Mayor. After his death in 1937 the business closed and the Corporation purchased the property, but demolition did not take place until after the Second World War.

# Westgate - part I

## The impact of street widening

Westgate is one of Ripon's ancient streets, mentioned as early as 1228 and periodically rebuilt over the centuries. Illustrations of the street however go back no further than the late 19thC when the first photographs were taken, but fortunately a number of these survive.

In 1900 Westgate had many shops and pubs which have long since disappeared. That process began with the decision by Ripon Corporation to widen the narrow streets of the town, and work started in Westgate early in 1903, setting back the properties on the north side of the street.

The first step was taken when Dennis Moss's upholsterer's and china shop on the corner with the Market Place was demolished, not without some danger to the public if a contemporary newspaper report is to be believed - apparently there was no scaffolding or hoarding, only a single workman in the street to warn passers-by.

The property was owned by Lord Ripon who sold off what was left of the building to Freeman Hardy and Willis. They erected the shoe shop there, although the attractive cupola seen in the photograph (c.1910) was regrettably taken down some years ago. Next to the shoe shop, at No.1 Westgate, was James Eden's greengrocer's shop.

It was to be another six years before the next stage in the widening process was agreed. In 1909 agreement was reached between the Corporation and W. H. Geldart over the compensation and rebuilding details relating to the new shop that

was to replace the *Alexandra* Hotel (named such in honour of the Princess of Wales by 1875 and formerly the *Coach and Horses*). The new structure with its balustraded roof can just be seen in the picture.

Next door is W. R. Reed's grocer's shop, as yet unaltered, taking advantage of the sudden difference in the building line to capitalise on advertising space! In 1910 however, it was to come down, leaving the *Green Dragon* next in the firing line.

Although increasingly worried about the cost of the widening scheme, the Corporation succeeded in reaching agreement with the new owners of the former pub (the licence having ceased), and two shops were to replace it. Henry Bulmer Rudd, chemist and photographer, was eventually to move into one of them where there is now the Spa Pharmacy.

And this was where the widening had to stop. Although there was some consultation with Dr Thomas Collier at No.5 next door it came to nothing, perhaps because the doctor would not lightly surrender the area between his railings and his front door, perhaps because the Corporation had had so many problems with the cost of its street widening programme it was losing interest, and civic attention turned elsewhere. At least in Westgate it was not impossible for the vehicles of the day to pass each other - and as the photograph reminds us, it was still the heyday of the bicycle!

## Westgate - Part II

### Changing appearances

These two views looking west were probably taken about 1900, immediately before the rebuilding in more imposing style of the Yorkshire Banking Company in 1900-1, later to become the Midland Bank, and now the HSBC. The manager then was John D. Waller. Two years later a start was made with the Corporation's scheme for widening Westgate by setting back buildings on the north side of the street, as described in the last article.

Properties on the south side of Westgate cannot be seen so clearly, but well down the street is the sign of the *Black Swan* hotel (licensee Henry Notley), the only one of Westgate's public houses to survive to this day. Like the others it is recorded from the early 19thC and is probably much older.

Nearer to the camera on the same side is the Temperance Hotel, managed at that time by Thomas Precious and often referred to by its former name of

Leake's Cocoa Rooms. Not visible are many other businesses including two more grocers, two butchers, two drapers, the shoe shop of Freeman, Hardy and Willis (soon to move), the 'mourning warehouse' of Peter Bray, and the shop of Henry Bulmer Rudd, chemist and photographer, who probably took this picture among many others of the town..

By 1917 his business had crossed the road to 4 Westgate, to occupy one of the new shops built on the site of the former *Green Dragon*.

Note that the absence of motor traffic made it possible to stand in the road in those days, though the hazard then was horse droppings!


## The Victoria Café

### Inn, ironmonger's, café, chemist

Boots long and low street frontage on the Market Place is eye-catching, but it is a replica (1977) of the elongated single-storey building with large upper windows and carriageway passage that previously stood here. That building however was largely a development of the mid-19thC. Before then, in the late 18thC, when its name was *The Minster Inn*, its appearance was very different as it consisted of two rather taller properties side by side, parts of which were found when the building was demolished in 1977. These parts were of considerable age - expert examination of the timbers revealed that part of the roof was of a rare type (crown post with cusped braces) and was probably late medieval in date. One of the great tie beams of this roof can still be seen against the wall in the carriageway.

The earliest documentary reference to the building so far known dates only from 1675, when it was the property of Alderman Roger Wright, a mercer who later became three times Mayor of Ripon. It was Wright who had established the long frontage of this site by acquiring the two adjacent properties that stood here. Wright died in 1712, and by 1747 the combined buildings had come into the possession of William Aislabie of Studley Royal.

By the late 18thC these structures had become the *York Minster Inn* and meetings were held here, including one in 1766 to discuss the building of Ripon's canal. It was still a hostelry in 1822 but within a few years (by 1829) drastic changes had taken place. The two buildings were merged into one and re-fronted with the large sash windows and carriageway arch that made it such a familiar sight in Victorian times. There was also a major change of use - from inn to ironmonger's, as it was

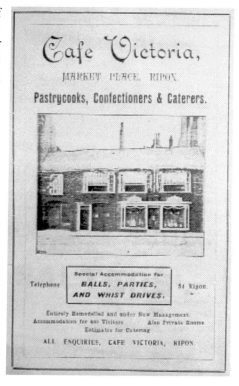

taken over by John Leyland and then by Henry Morton, an enterprising and successful businessman who, like Roger Wright before him, was to be three times Mayor of Ripon (1851-4). The tunnel arch, which seems to have included a public right of way, no doubt gave access to storage and workshop buildings at the rear.

The ironmonger's business continued there for the rest of the century, passing in 1839 to Morton's former apprentice and later partner Thomas Kendall (Mayor in 1859-60), and then by the 1870s to William Parkinson and later Benjamin Wigglesworth (1897). In 1898 the Marquess of Ripon sold the property to the Phoenix Improvement Company, whilst retaining upstairs use for the 'Ripon Club', an esoteric group thought still to survive to our own day.

The Edwardian Age was to see ownership pass to the new Café Victoria (Ripon) Ltd., which was to flourish in the years to come; Assembly Rooms were built at the rear for meetings and social events, and it became a very popular nightspot both before and after the Second World War, offering an alternative to the Lawrence Café and Ballroom.

However, by the 1970s it was threatened with redevelopment, and in 1975 planning consent was given for it to become a branch of Boots. One condition was that the existing facade be retained, but as reconstruction was taking place, the architects deemed that the frontage was unstable and must be demolished. The Planning Authority insisted however that it should be rebuilt as a replica of its predecessor, creating the effect that we see today.

# The *George and Dragon*

## Another of Ripon's lost pubs

In the second half of the 20thC, as social habits changed, many long-established public houses closed down in Ripon as elsewhere, and several of these were around the Market Place. At one time both the *York Minster Inn* (now Boots) and the *George and Dragon* (now Superdrug) flourished on the west side of the Square, and the latter survived until quite recent times.

Once known as the *George*, it is recorded as early as 1731, when its owner, Jane Robinson, sold it to John Forster of Runswick, the son of a cousin, who kept it for the next thirty years. It later passed to one John Morley, who in 1808 sold it to Richard Delicate, and it was he who decided to change its name from the *George* to the *George and Dragon* (by 1822). Shortly afterwards Delicate died, aged 59, in 1828.

The plan was for the pub to pass to his son Richard Delicate junior, but as he was only eight, his cousin Jeremiah took over until Richard was old enough to run it himself. However, when that time came, Richard died of consumption in 1843 and his baby son was left the pub in trust.

George Walbank was pub landlord in 1848, but ten years later Ann Blakeborough was in charge, to be followed by James Hanby in the 1860s. Big changes however were soon to come, when the next landlord Anthony Bland bought the property from Richard Delicate's family in 1876 and set about rebuilding it in the 1880s.

The 1881 census reveals full details of Anthony Bland's family at the *George and Dragon*. He had been born at Kirkby Malzeard and was 56 that year. His wife Mary from Carlsmoor was five years younger, and was mother to four sons and two daughters who lived with them, their ages ranging from 24 to 10. On the day of the census there were also four lodgers staying there as well as a servant.

Ten years later Anthony Bland was dead, but the inn was being run by his widow Mary, with the help of her family. The following year, however, she sold

it to John Nicholson, and it was his premises, as owner and licensee, that were described in a fascinating document of 1901, a survey of all the town's public houses at the start of the 20thC. The *George and Dragon* is described as a free house, able to accommodate as many as 180 diners at a time, with seven bedrooms for visitors.

There was a front entrance from the Square, and two side entrances under the archway which led through to a yard with coach house and stabling for 18 horses (where William Hill's now stands)

John Nicholson was the last of the pub's private owners - shortly before the First World War he sold it to John Smith's Tadcaster Brewery and the *George and Dragon* remained in brewery hands thereafter. Its long history came to a sad and contentious end, however, in 1986 when the decision was made to close the pub (despite a petition from 750 angry regulars) and convert it to more profitable retail use. So another of Ripon's centuries-old hostelries disappeared, a victim of changing economic forces.

# Fishergate

## More street widening and yet another lost pub

Again the theme is street-widening, with attention now turning to Fishergate, another of Ripon's ancient thoroughfares, appearing on a map of 1733 and no doubt as old as the medieval Market Place itself.

In Edwardian times, every street had its pub or pubs, and Fishergate was no exception. The *Wheat Sheaf* on the site of present day Woolworth's had already come and gone by 1900, leaving local trade to the *Grapes* inn on the corner of Fishergate and Lavender Alley, and here, about 1905, we see a group of gents (one definitely under age) apparently waiting for opening time.

The *Grapes* is recorded from the 1830s and before then was known as the *Three Tuns*. However Arthur J. Hirst was to prove to be the last of the landlords - the street was being steadily widened from the Market Place end, and the beleaguered *Grapes* was left out on a limb, as the photograph shows. After the usual dispute over compensation was finally settled, demolition followed (1906) and the debris was removed in two days, although the inn sign is thought still to survive in safe storage.

Among the shops of Fishergate in Edwardian times was Hemsworth's antiques business, the snow covered sign of which can be seen in the picture. William Hemsworth was later Mayor of Ripon for three successive years (1922-5) and carried out a major restoration of the Wakeman's House. In the inter-war years his shop was regularly visited by Queen Mary.

On the east side of the road, Raper's footwear shop on the corner with Market Place North lost a third of the building through the widening process,

but the main casualty was the unlikely block of terraced cottages which occupied the rest of that side of the street up to the *Grapes* inn. Beyond the *Grapes* in 1901 was Crouch & Co., fishmonger and game dealer, and Richard Guy, tailor and outfitter.

On the west side of the road was an assortment of shops including Bilton the shoemaker (seen in the picture), Thomas Mountain, coach builder and cab proprietor, Tomlinson's which sold ham and bacon, Jackson's drapers and bespoke tailors, and John Gardam the watchmaker.

Fishergate is still quite narrow even today, but times and shopping patterns have changed, as reflected in its present day multiples and charity shops.

## Hebden's Corner

### A long-established local family with links world-wide

As noted in the article on Fishergate, the demolition of the *Grapes Inn* (1906) marked the end of street widening in this part of the town, so the picture accompanying this article, clearly showing the bunch of grapes sign, is therefore pre-1906. It is actually pre-1902, since demolition began in that year of the elongated island of property (still seen here) between Middle Street and Queen Street.

It does in fact date to about 1900, and was probably taken early in the morning to avoid the traffic - even so there are one or two curious early risers about. It shows Hebden's ironmonger's shop standing proudly at the junction of Fishergate and Old Market Place, a location popularly known as Hebden's Corner. Its postal address was actually 9 Old Market Place and the ironmonger was James Hebden, born at Grantley, aged 54 in 1901, and still running the business as late as 1922. In later years the shop became Boots the Chemist and is now the Abbey National.

What do we know about Hebden family history? Their complex story can be traced right back to the Middle Ages. The list of Wakemen (to 1604) contains the name Hebden six times - it occurs more often than any other surname. The silver badge of Thomas Hebden, Wakeman in 1576, still survives on the baldric in the Town Hall.

Later a William Hebden was Mayor in 1669; his family left Ripon for Gainsborough and London where we find another William Hebden a blacksmith at Woolwich in the 1730s, and Darcy Hebden, an officer who served in the Battle of Dettingen in 1743, the last battle in which a British monarch led his troops into action.

In the early 17thC another branch of the family moved to Sawley, from where later descendants migrated to Appletreewick to prosper in farming and innkeeping; whilst later still two Hebden brothers were running cotton-spinning mills at Bolton in Lancashire in the mid/late 19thC. Another descendant became a schoolmaster at Lofthouse in the late 18thC, whilst his son went to London and two of his grandsons emigrated to Australia.

Other Hebdens settled in the Grantley area, giving rise to the Hebden tanners and maltsters at Braisty Woods, the last of whom died at Meerut, India in 1841 whilst serving with the 16th Lancers. His widowed sister was the first and only lady lighthouse keeper at Wellington in New Zealand.

Of those remaining at Grantley, James Hebden, born in 1847, was the founder of the ironmongery business in Old Market Place.

His eldest son Herbert (b.1881) was killed in the First World War, leaving a son who travelled worldwide for the War Graves Commission after the Second World War and then retired to Australia where he recently celebrated his Diamond Wedding anniversary, and hopes to celebrate his 90th birthday later in 2004. As the Hebdens show, family history can be both complicated and fascinating.

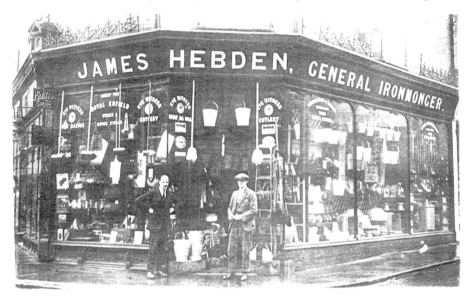

# The *Black Bull*

## Welcoming travellers over the centuries

The Old Market Place is dominated by the *Black Bull*, and has been for at least 200 years - it is indeed one of Ripon's ancient hostelries. Looked at carefully from the Square, the roof-line of the inn suggests that it is a merger of two properties, but it is more likely in fact that what we see is the piecemeal rebuilding of a large and sumptuous hall-house dating back to Tudor times - the western part certainly contains extensive timber framing of the 16th and 17thC. However, the windows, doors, stairs, rooms and even outside walls have been much altered over the years, evidence of the *Black Bull*'s long and active life.

The earliest landlord who has so far come to light was William Hodgson, recorded in 1801 and again in 1811. By 1826 William Milner was in charge, and then from the late 1830s the Beaumonts, first Thomas and then in the 1850s, Margaret, no doubt his widow. This period, the early 19thC, must have been the most active and exciting time in the history of the *Black Bull*, since it was then that along with the *Unicorn* it served as one of the town's two great coaching inns.

In the late 1820s, the *Courier* stage coach set off at 7.00 am daily from the *Black Bull* on its way to Harrogate and Leeds, returning in the evening, whilst the *Highflier* called three times a week as it travelled between York and Middleham. There was even a stage coach service that operated three times a week to Redcar "during the bathing season", returning passengers the next day.

Stops at the coaching inns were not just to pick up or put down passengers but also to change horses, and horses required extensive stabling. A plan of the period reveals a significant increase in stabling around the Black Bull Yard in the early 19thC, especially along its west side. The inn also served as a depot for carrier services in those days, such as Pickersgill of Leeming Lane - goods would be left for regular and early delivery to Leeds, Leyburn and even Newcastle and London.

The arrival of the railway in 1848 had a devastating impact on the long distance stage coaches which were too slow to compete, but the *Courier* even in the 1850s continued to offer a passenger service to Middleham every evening. For a while the *Black Bull* ran an omnibus service to the railway station, but soon left this to others. The pace of life, which had once been hectic, must definitely have slackened for the rest of the 19thC.

A detailed picture of the *Black Bull* at the time of Queen Victoria's death is given in the Magistrates' Survey of 1901. The then landlord was John Mackley, and the facilities he offered were reminiscent of the Coaching Era - food as well as drink, overnight accommodation for 30, and the capacity to feed 70 diners at a time. Interestingly, a large coach-house is mentioned, and stabling (though dilapidated) for 26 horses.

Since that time the stables have disappeared to make way for cars, and the *Black Bull* has flourished as a friendly drinking house for students and locals. It is also a popular venue on market and race days. It has a proud history, and is certainly one of the city's 'ancient charms'.


# The Old Market Place - Part I

### The City's most historic corner

This late 19thC view of the cobbled Old Market Place shows striking differences from that scene today, but the hostelries on either side of the picture provide helpful reference points. Most easily recognizable is the *Black Bull* on the left, then already centuries old and much used by long distance stage coaches until the coming of the railway (1848) sent this trade into terminal decline.

In the centre of the picture is a curious three-bay structure with gable ends facing the street and a flight of stone steps up to one of the doors. This was clearly an ancient building, and the cement render no doubt concealed a framework of timbers similar to that of the Wakeman's House. As the street signs indicate, the whole building was then part of Finkle Street and included Harrison the butcher, still today a well-known name in that part of town.

Research reveals that Harrison's business survived the most extraordinary tribulations in those days. Sometime about 1870 Edward Harrison had moved from Low Skellgate to Finkle Street, as seen in the picture, but his shop was demolished in1893 to make way for the Mechanics' Institute (now the Post Office). He migrated to 1 Middle Street, an elongated block of properties that in those days separated Middle Street from Queen Street. However, this shop itself was soon under threat of demolition, and by 1905 all the units had gone, giving Queen Street its present wide appearance. Rayner's the drapers was the last shop to go.

Meanwhile Harrison's had returned to Finkle Street, though now to No. 8, much further along towards Allhallowgate, and there the business stayed until again the premises had to come down, on this occasion as part of the post-World

War II street clearance that made way for the large block of flats on the corner. This time Harrison's moved along into one of the few surviving shop units at the south end of the street, the present No. 3.

The twin-gabled building in the picture carries the name H. Cooper, identifying the rope and twine business of Helen Cooper (d. 1889) which she ran there as a widow for 40 years. There was a Rope Walk in the yard at the rear. Earlier members of the Cooper family had long been active in the rope-making trade in this part of the town. By 1912 however, these premises (4 Old Market Place) had not only changed hands but had been rebuilt, as William Benson the ironmonger moved there from 7 King Street.

Finally, towering over the twin gables, is the *Star Hotel*, recorded as early as 1801 and still going strong today (with altered windows) as the *Hornblower Tavern*. Run in 1901 by Margaret Chapman, it is described in some detail in a magistrates' survey of pubs in that year. It was then owned by Hepworth's Brewery of Bondgate and had accommodation for six travellers and stables for 20 horses. The

magistrates however noted with disapproval that the 'tenant encourages drinking by young lads'.

The medieval origins of the Old Market Place are still unclear, but it was described as 'old' even in 1450, and it is easy toforget how its appearance must have changed many times over the centuries, unrecorded until the advent of the camera.

## Old Market Place - Part II

### Cutting out the Middle (Street) men

The view of the Old Market Place in the previous article is extended here as the camera pans round to the right and focuses on that elongated island of properties which once connected the Old Market Place to the Market Place proper. Pictures of Rayner's frontage at the latter end are now well known, but here we have a view of the less familiar north end, where Charles Wyatt had his shop at the time of the death of Queen Victoria (1901).

Charles Wyatt dealt in mounting, framing and gilding pictures for people to hang in their houses; perhaps he had also been responsible for the ornate weather vane on the roof. Because of the way his shop faced, its postal address was actually 14 Old Market Place, but it was to make no difference when the decision was taken in 1902 to demolish the whole block and widen the street. By 1904 all the shops had gone except for Rayner's, and Wyatt had moved his business to 13 Fishergate where, working with his son, he continued up to the First World War.

Other traders in that doomed central block in 1900 were Edward Harrison the butcher (see previous article), plus two other butchers (Eastman Ltd. and C. Prest). There was also a bootmaker (Roberts), a ladies & children's outfitter (Miss Eliza Burton), a fruiterer and game dealer (T. Horsman), and William Harrison the hairdresser, whose barber's pole can just be seen in the picture.

Fifty years earlier, long before Rayner's took it over, the end shop looking onto the Square had been run by Thomas Walker and Robert Aslin, wholesale hosiers and lace dealers. Perhaps being positioned close to so many pubs led teetotal Thomas Walker to hate the demon drink, because on his deathbed (1858) he made a substantial donation of £100 to start a fund for the building of a Temperance Hall. The site chosen was on Duck Hill, other money began to flow in, and soon an Assembly Hall with committee room and caretaker's house had been erected there (1859). By 1880 all the debt had been cleared, but temperance as a cause was soon to be on the wane, and from the time of the Great War the building was being put to other uses - by soldiers, by Scouts and most recently as the Ripon Small Shops Arcade.

To the left of Wyatt's shop can be seen the narrow entrance to Queen Street, which a hundred years earlier was known as Ripon's shambles (or butchers' row) and also as Ratten Row. In 1900 the shop with the gable end to the street was Snowden's the confectioner; beyond it was James Watkin, clothier and boot dealer. For those who ventured further into this claustrophobic street there was the *Yorkshire Hussar* (not in the picture) where John Smith's beer could be drunk standing at the bar. The magistrates' survey of 1901 tells us that singing took place there on a Saturday night - perhaps an early form of karaoke?

The effect of removing the central block of property was to merge two ancient streets into one very wide avenue, and one name - inevitably Middle Street - had to go. All those businesses formerly on the west side of Middle Street now found themselves with Queen Street addresses and would have had to change their bill heads accordingly. Such was the price of progress!

# J. Rayner

## No man is an island

These photographs show the final stages of the destruction of that elongated block of property that separated Middle Street from Queen Street at the beginning of the Edwardian period, and had done so no doubt since medieval times.

Beginning in 1902 the street-widening programme was done piecemeal as negotiations with the individual property owners proceeded smoothly, but difficulties were encountered with the shop at the south end of the block, No.16 Market Place, where the owner John Rayner, a draper, was not impressed by the amount of compensation offered and refused to co-operate.

As a result his shop eventually came to be left in a singularly isolated position as the pictures show, though business appears to have continued as usual, with the back wall of what had become Ripon's quaintest shop hurriedly transformed into an advertising opportunity - *'Reliable Fashionable Goods at Reasonable Prices'*.

This situation however could not last, and in 1905 compensation of nearly £5000 was agreed after arbitration. The building came down, Rayner's relocated to new premises close by, and Queen Street came into being basically as it is today - easily the widest street leading into the Market Place.

# Moss

## A complicated story behind a local business name

One of the most interesting pieces of furniture in the Town Hall is the circular tilt-top breakfast table which stands in a corner of the Mayor's Parlour. Made of mahogany and rosewood, it follows the usual style of such tables by having a central pedestal and elegant cabriole legs. For easy storage (after breakfast) the top folded down vertically to economise on space.

The particular interest of this fine antique is that it was made locally - notably by William Moss, joiner and cabinet maker, in his workshop on the Market Place which stood where Stead and Simpson now sell their footwear. William Moss was born in 1813, the son of Henry Moss and Elizabeth Topham. Henry was a joiner in Kirkgatehead, and his son followed in father's footsteps, but graduated to become joiner *and* cabinet maker with a workshop on the Square. William and his wife Ann had several children in the 1840s, and it is probably to this period that the table dates.

A City Councillor in the 1850s, he continued to head the business into the 1860s, but by the time of the 1881 Census, control had passed to William's younger brother Henry, aged 62 and recorded as a cabinet maker employing a man and a boy. By then William, now a widower, had moved to Ure Bank Terrace and was running Moss's Albion Varnish Works with his two sons. One of them, William junior, eventually inherited the business and went on in later years to serve two terms as Mayor of Ripon (1902-4). He died in 1930, and the Varnish Works was not long to survive him.

The other branch of the Moss family, now represented by Dennis Moss, continued to occupy their Market Place premises until the very end of the 19thC, but by then, in addition to cabinet making, they had branched out into ceramics - the workshop had become a china shop selling Goss and other souvenir items bearing the Ripon shield; the tourist trade had arrived. Even more drastic change came in 1903 when the shop was demolished and rebuilt to allow work to begin on the widening of Westgate. By that time however the Moss family had given up the site which had been acquired by Freeman, Hardy and Willis and turned into a shoe shop.

However, there was now a new Moss presence in Ripon. W.B. Moss & Sons Ltd, grocers from Hitchin, had opened a branch in Queen Street, and their shop came to mark the entrance to Moss's Arcade (1899). The Manager of this well known store was Sidney George Moss who deserves credit for stepping in to buy and save the dilapidated Wakeman's House in 1915 which he later sold on to the Corporation for restoration. He served as Mayor in 1929/30.

The business was eventually sold in 1961 and Moss's Arcade demolished two years later, although the name has been preserved for the road leading to the Bus Station. Forty years on, Ripon has gained a new shopping arcade on the same side of the Square.

# The *Crown Hotel*

## An embarrassing episode for the Mayor

Were it not for the plaque on the wall, the hundreds of people who go through Morrison's Arcade each week would have little idea that an inn stood on this site only a hundred years ago. It was the *Crown Hotel*, a fine imposing building with bay windows and a balcony over the archway, as the picture shows. But two hundred years earlier it had been known as the *White Hart*, and it first attracted public attention in less than auspicious circumstances.

In 1686 the then proprietor was Christopher Hunton, who enjoyed the honour of becoming Mayor of Ripon in that year. One of the Mayor's main responsibilities was to look after the town silver, especially the Charter Horn with its silver badges, but for a publican to put it on display in his pub was to tempt providence. Various items went missing, Hunton had to pay twenty shillings in recompense to the Corporation, and attempts were later made by John Aislabie and others

to recover the lost items. (Exactly three hundred years later, in 1986, the city silver again fell victim to theft, this time from the Town Hall).

The *White Hart* passed first to Hunton's descendants, his son and his grandson, and then to others. It was probably late in the 18thC that it was rebuilt from timber to brick and stone, with major extensions added at the rear. Appropriately it was renamed the *New Inn*, but by 1811 it had changed name again to the *Crown and Anchor* and had become part of the Studley Royal estate. From the end of the 1830s it was run for over fifty years by the Blacker family, and it came simply to be known as the *Crown*.

A survey of licensed houses in 1901 revealed that it had twelve bedrooms for visitors, stabling for 20 horses, and it could dine 150. By then it was owned by the Marquess of Ripon, but in 1903 it passed to Sir Christopher Furness, as part of a major hotel development scheme for the south-east side of the Square that also involved Harrison's and the *Unicorn*. This however (fortunately!) never happened, being replaced by the Spa project which included the building of a new hotel, and in 1907 the *Crown* closed.

After being a hostelry for at least 300 years, the building then became a motor works when Croft and Blackburn moved there in 1908 and later acquired the ownership (1919). Their petrol pumps on the Market Place forecourt were to be a familiar sight for many years until the property was bought by William Morrison Supermarkets in 1974. Much of the façade of the ancient hostelry was retained, and the *Crown* sign went into safe storage in the rear of the Wakeman's House, from whence it emerged to return to its original location in 2001.

## W. Harrison

### The Ripon Millenary Record: how it came to be written

Over the years much has been written about the history of Ripon, but without doubt the fullest and most detailed account is the famous *Ripon Millenary Book*, a hefty tome that was published in 1892 primarily to describe the various goings-on during the Millenary Festival of 1886, but for posterity its greatest value lies in the historical information presented in the second half of the book. For over a hundred years now this has been an invaluable source of often obscure yet fascinating detail for local historians, and surviving copies of the book are still much sought after.

The driving force behind both the 1886 Festival and the publication of this great work was the printer and bookbinder William Harrison whose business is still very much in operation today. At the age of 21 he had taken over on the death of his father (also a William) in 1867, and the younger William shared his father's interest in local history and matters antiquarian. Educated at the Grammar School, he married Annabella Wells, daughter of William Wells the wine and spirits merchant. In 1914 their only son, William Wells Harrison, was taken into partnership, and the same year he succeeded to the whole business when his father died.

Harrison's printing business started up in 1840, but the premises had already been used for that purpose for some time, first by Thomas Langdale (by 1813) and then by John Linney (1836-40). By the mid-19thC Harrison's also housed the office of the *Ripon Chronicle*, a forerunner of the present-day Gazette.

As the picture shows, and as anyone can still clearly see looking at Harrison's from across the road, the shop actually takes up only half of a fine 18thC building (the windows are later) with a central passageway. The southern half of the building belongs to the *Unicorn* (Tom Crudd's bar) and has done so for many years. The explanation of this anomalous state of affairs is still not fully understood, but it seems that when the Kirkby family, who built and owned the whole building in the mid-18thC, sold it to John Ullithorne in 1769, he immediately sold on the southern half to Sarah Haddon of the *Unicorn*. For many years however it remained a separate unit run as a grocer's shop before being absorbed into the *Unicorn* by Robert Collinson in the mid-1870s.

William Harrison's task of producing a major study of Ripon's history was no doubt inspired by the 1886 Festival, but it was to take several years of painstaking work to produce (1892) and involved a number of contributors - chief among them the Rev. W. C. Lukis and William Grainge. As editor, William Harrison also drew on his father's historical notes and on the research work of the former local historian John Richard Walbran.

So valuable did the Millenary book prove in the years to come that it was decided a century later during the 1986 Festival to produce a sequel that would cover the history of Ripon during the years that had elapsed since the original publication. The result was another team effort, *A Ripon Record 1887-1986*, now out of print but still much used by those probing the City's past in the century of the two World Wars.

# The *Unicorn Hotel*

## The hotel at the city centre

The name of the *Unicorn Inn* is recorded in use from the early 17thC. It may in fact date back much earlier to medieval times when unicorns were regarded as fabulous beasts whose horns (hard to come by) when made into drinking cups were proof against all poisons. But it is also possible that the inn's name was not adopted until James I's reign when the unicorn was added to the Royal Coat of Arms and the king paid Ripon a personal visit (1617).

A scarcely less important visitor a few years later was Edward Alleyn, a theatre actor-manager from London who became Keeper of the King's Beasts and then went on to found Dulwich College. In July 1626 he signed legal papers at the *Unicorn* in Ripon, providing the earliest record so far found of the inn's name. At that time it was run by Margaret Turner who had already been twice widowed, and had survived plague in the town in 1625.

After her death in 1646 the inn came into the possession of the Porter family, father then son, but from the 1690s it fell into fragmented ownership for nearly 50 years. In 1697 Ripon was visited by the much travelled Celia Fiennes who recorded in her diary that in Ripon "some of the inns are very dear to strangers that they can impose on" - hopefully the *Unicorn* was not one of these! Mine host at the

*Unicorn* during Queen Anne's reign was Francis Cowling, who was regularly paid by the Corporation to supply drinks 'at the Cross' to celebrate Marlborough's victories and later the accession of George I (8s. 4d for five quarts of wine).

In 1744 the property was reunited into a single ownership, to be run by William and Sarah Haddon, and the Haddon family was to control the affairs of the *Unicorn* for the rest of the century. Nearly all the buildings around the Square were upgraded from timber framing to brick in the 18thC, and the evidence for the *Unicorn* suggests that this happened about 1770 and was the work of Sarah Haddon, by now a widow.

It was in those years that the *Unicorn* achieved widespread if not national fame through the exploits of Tom Crudd, who as 'Boots' had the task of helping travellers remove their outdoor footwear and put on slippers. Crudd had a natural 'Mr. Punch' face and his party trick was to ask for a coin which he then held betwixt nose and chin, to the great merriment of the visitors. But Crudd kept the coin and so had the last laugh!

During the early years of the Napoleonic War, John Fairgray was innkeeper - but not owner - of the *Unicorn*. He went on to become Mayor of Ripon and his portrait still hangs in the Mayor's Parlour. In 1805 the Ripon Loyal Volunteer Corps entertained their colonel at the *Unicorn*, the dinner ending "with the utmost conviviality and mirth". But only a few years later Ripon innkeepers were complaining bitterly at having a regiment of regular infantry billeted upon them. In the early 19thC the *Unicorn* was a busy place, servicing stage coaches and private carriages and favoured for a variety of events and meetings. In 1821 the inn became part of the Studley Royal estate and was soon serving as the base of the Tory Party during local elections, whilst victory at the polls justified "splendid dinners" such as that provided by "Mr Thwaites, the spirited landlord of the *Unicorn*" in 1835.

From the early 1860s until his death in 1889, Robert Ellington Collinson was the highly regarded landlord who managed to find time also to be Mayor of Ripon for four consecutive years (1876-80). He was followed in the 1890s by Bernard and Elizabeth Evans. In 1902 the Studley Estate relinquished ownership of the *Unicorn* after which it passed through various hands - including Hepworth's and Vaux Breweries - before being acquired by David and Maureen Small in 1983.

# J. B. Parkin

### Ripon's earliest chemist's shop?

By the early 19thC the term *apothecary* had given way to *chemist* for those whose occupation was selling drugs and potions to the public for their alleged benefit. Despite advances in medical science there were still many quack cures available even in late Victorian times (e.g. *Dr. Rooke's Solar Elixir*) and plenty of people ready to try them. Less controversial perhaps were the toothpastes and cold creams which were sold in attractive small pots, their lids transfer-printed with details of the product and the vendor.

Ripon had its own chemists, then as now, and one of them, Joseph Brooks Parkin became Mayor of the city in 1892. Parkin had been born in 1839 at Bishop Thornton, one of the several children of the school master of Markington.

Young Parkin attended Ripon Grammar School and then became apprenticed to John Brown, a chemist in Westgate, who described himself in a trade directory of 1861 as "patent medicine vendor and sole agent for Anderton's artificial manures".

In 1867, aged 28, Parkin set up his own business, choosing premises in Kirkgatehead, and probably taking over the chemist's shop previously run for decades by John Anderson (it was later claimed a chemist's shop had been there since 1720). A few years later the 1881 census reveals details of his family - his wife Elizabeth and three children Katherine (12), Frederic (11) and Lilian (8) - but an entry in the Cathedral burial register indicates that his first wife, Eliza, the mother of his children, had died in 1877 after which time he re-married.

In the 1870s Joseph Parkin became a member of the City Corporation and later an Alderman. He was a busy man - a magistrate, a Governor of the Grammar School at the time of its move out to Bishopton, a churchwarden at the Cathedral, and Chairman of Jepson's Hospital in Water Skellgate. In 1892 he became Mayor, and the highlight of his year of office was no doubt presiding over the celebrations to mark the Royal Wedding of the Duke of York (later George V) to Princess Mary of Teck (later Queen Mary) in July 1893. The shops closed at lunchtime on the wedding day, and the Square filled with a great throng of children's groups, all looking toward the Town Hall, but Mayor Parkin with his chain of office was down there with them. The streets were specially decorated, the workhouse inmates given roast beef and plum pudding, and the royal couple were sent a silver horn and a copy of the *Ripon Millenary*.

A few years later, in 1896, Parkin died suddenly while on holiday in Southport, and the shop passed to his son. It was still listed as *Parkin and Son* in a trade directory of 1901, but by 1908 it had been taken over by one Ralph Osborn-Beacher, who was quick to advertise it as "the second oldest Chemist's shop in England, with a reputation of over 200 years". A speciality of the shop was 'Ye Olde Ripon Lavender Water'. However, time was about to run out. After the First World War the shop (No.1 Kirkgate) became Blades ironmongers (with the trade shovel on the wall), after which the Stainton family ran a business there for several decades. It then became *Houseproud* for some fifteen years, and a further change of use has since taken place.

# The St. Wilfrid Procession

## From humble beginnings

This print of the Wilfrid Procession in Kirkgate was published in the London Illustrated News in 1844 and it shows some distinct differences from the procession nowadays. Firstly, the figure of St Wilfrid is revealed by its stiffness to be an effigy, not a man, and his costume is not that of a bishop but of an 18thC gentleman. Nor do his attendants wear monks' habits but the ordinary dress of

ST WILFRID FESTIVAL, RIPON.

the day, and two of them with flute and fiddle hardly resemble the Band of today. However the drum to which contemporaries refer appears to be missing.

The procession seems to be coming away from the cathedral rather than going to it, as happens nowadays. Was it really like this or did the illustrator alter the scene to get a better picture with the cathedral in the background? And of course instead of the decorated floats and classic cars that now follow St Wilfrid, there is only a crowd of curious pedestrians. One figure will be familiar - the man collecting donations - but it is unlikely that the proceeds at that time went to charity. More probably it found its way to local innkeepers as the festival was notorious for its drunkenness.

What can we learn of the street itself? On the south side can be seen the shop of George Bell, the boot and shoe maker, whilst on the north side there is the way through to Robert Whitton's monumental stonemason's yard and to the back of the *Unicorn*. Beyond are William John Pinn's grocery shop and Durham's the draper, whilst at the end of the street can be seen the *Minster Inn* (innkeeper John Hunton).

In Kirkgate at that time there were three boot and shoe makers, three bakers and confectioners, and three tailors, as well as hat-makers, joiners, a chemist and a butcher, to mention just a few others; and the police station was where the Gazette office now is. Adding to the importance of the street at this time was the fact that Ripon Corporation met there having been debarred from the Town Hall since 1835 by its then owner Mrs. Lawrence of Studley Royal, since she objected to accommodating newly-elected Whig members. In 1845 however she died, and the Corporation was back in the Town Hall within a few years.

All in all Kirkgate was a very different street then compared with today, being far more geared to local rather than visitor needs, and it was to be many years before the type of business changed significantly. But aspects of the procession had altered dramatically within three years. By 1847 the effigy had been replaced by a man, and he was dressed in the cope and mitre of a bishop. The timing too had been changed - from August 17 in 1844 to July 31 in 1847, about the date that it takes place today.

The reason for this was commercial. As well as having the Wilfrid Procession on the third Saturday of August there had also been a race meeting, but this suffered from a clash with a race meeting in York. Concerned at the likely loss of custom, traders now insisted that the date be changed to avoid this, and the Race Committee agreed. But not everyone in Ripon did, and for some years there were two Wilfrid Processions! By Edwardian times the City Band had come to lead the procession, and the colourful floats were added in the 1960s.

# The *Royal Oak*

## A town tavern with right royal roots?

The *Royal Oak* is one of the oldest established hostelries in Ripon, and its name suggests that it may even date back to the late 17thC when there was a resurgence of royalist feeling after Cromwell's rule and the monarchy was restored in the person of Charles II. As a youth the young Prince Charles had hidden as a fugitive in an oak tree to avoid capture after losing the battle of Worcester (1651), and that tree became thereafter a symbol of support for the *Crown*.

The imposing building that we see today however is a later rebuilding, dating almost certainly to the 18thC with a doorframe and architectural details of that century, and the earliest information to survive regarding the owners of the property also comes from that period. William Askwith, a brewer who was Mayor of Ripon in 1758, and again in 1769, owned properties in Kirkgate which included the *Royal Oak*, and it was there that meetings were held (1766) to discuss and plan the construction of Ripon's canal.

William Askwith died in 1776 and was succeeded by his son, also called William and then aged 36. This younger William turned out to be a local benefactor who was responsible in that very year for a major improvement to the town's water supply when he arranged for water from the river Skell to be pumped up Duck Hill. We are told that before this, water was carried on horseback from house to house in leather bags. Askwith arranged for an engine to be constructed in the

Archbishop of York's mill at the foot of Duck Hill, and it was water from the mill race that was then pumped up to the town centre in wooden pipes (later replaced with lead pipes, and then iron).

This system provided the town with water until the 1860s when it was superseded by a major new municipal waterworks on the banks of the Ure near North Bridge. Askwith's scheme had no doubt been much appreciated by the townsfolk, but in those days water in the open mill race running through the town was no doubt contaminated, and in a dry summer there would have been little water to spare if the mill wheels were also to keep turning.

Askwith, like his father, went on to become Mayor (1782), and survived until 1814, but by 1801 he had been replaced as the proprietor of the *Royal Oak* by Thomas Wood, and the tavern was to be run first by Thomas, and then for the next 50 years by his widow (?) Elizabeth Wood. From the late 1850s however it changed hands more frequently, and by the end of the 19thC the proprietor of the *Royal Oak Commercial Hotel* was John William Hewson.

Interesting information is given in the Magistrates' Survey of Licensed Houses carried out in 1901, by which time the *Royal Oak* was owned by the Marquess of Ripon. It had a large dining room that could seat 60; there was sleeping accommodation for 14 persons, a coach house, and stabling for nearly 30 horses. As with other public houses there were problems with the drains, but overall the report was very favourable.

Over the next hundred years the *Royal Oak* was to survive the tumultuous times of the 20thC and now flourishes under capable management, enjoying royal patronage and an established clientele of appreciative regulars.

# The Old Courthouse

### From convicts to customers

This important and interesting building, recently an antiques shop standing in an enclosed yard off Minster Road, attracts many visitors in the summer months who cannot fail to detect there the atmosphere of an ancient past. Built as an ecclesiastical courthouse in the Middle Ages to hold the Minster's Canon Fee Court, its stone shell and some of the roof timbers survive from that period despite the doors and windows having been much altered since.

Upstairs at the northern end was the courtroom, reached by an outside staircase, with service and living rooms to the south, and a half-timbered extension bearing the possibly original date of 1613. Cells made up the ground floor and some of their features such as window bars still survive.

After the Reformation, control of the building passed from the Church to the local magistrates, and by the 18thC it was serving as the Gaol for the Liberty of Ripon, with its own resident salaried Gaoler. At one time his name ironically was Idle, whilst another, John Foxton (1794), was sacked and whipped around the Market Place for stealing the Dean's hay from the garth next door. Whipping with

a cat o' nine tails took place on Market Day as it was intended to be a public spectacle.

In the Gaol was incarcerated a variety of debtors and felons as well as prisoners on remand. Occasionally one escaped. A 'Wanted' poster of 1801, offering a reward, graphically described the escapee, 19 year old James Smith, as having sunken eyes, a small mouth and thin lips. He was also "rather bow-legged and in walking turns in his Toes a little". Whether this unsparing description led to his recapture is not known.

Prisoners were charged fees for a bed and bedsheets, though a shared bed came at a reduced rate! The prison population fluctuated but generally appears to have been quite small - three male debtors only in 1779, and no one at all in 1782.

The Gaol was visited by the great prison reformer John Howard in 1775 and by James Neild in 1812. It was not the worst prison that they visited by any means, but seems to have been in a continually dilapidated condition. However, the law was now demanding higher prison standards and in 1816 felons were transferred to the newly extended House of Correction in St. Marygate, leaving the Old Courthouse simply as a Debtors Prison, where the inmates were detained until they (or their families) paid their debts. It continued as such until the death of the last Gaoler, Thomas Harrison, in the 1850s when it was closed (as were other Debtors' prisons) and it has remained a private dwelling since.

The 20thC was to bring the greatest threat to the building since it was first built. In 1935 it was agreed that the dual carriageway Ripon Relief Road should follow the line of Bedern Bank (widened), divide Kirkgate from the Cathedral, and then proceed northwards across the site of the demolished Old Court House. This disastrous scheme was not abandoned until the late 1960s by which time the Bedern Bank properties had been demolished - but fortunately not Ripon's one-time Liberty Gaol.

# The Courthouse

## Now tourists go to court

Once buzzing with magistrates' business, Ripon's historic courtroom still retains much of its original character - so much so that it has been used as a stage set for the *Heartbeat* series on television. Such reconstructions of legal proceedings have of course taken over from the real thing since the decision was taken in 1998 to close the courthouse as an economy measure, despite the fact that a major extension to the building had been added less than twenty years earlier. However, relocating the Cathedral offices there does at least mean that the Courthouse is now in daily use, and the famous Courtroom can be seen by many visitors on Ripon's Law and Order Trail.

Compared with the Cathedral, the Courtroom is quite a modern building, having been constructed as recently as 1830, replacing the Common Hall, an inadequate structure of similar purpose which had once been part of the Archbishop's Palace which stood hereabouts. The architect was Grunwell, the builder was Michael Foxton, and the style Classical, as the fine pedimented doorway reminds us. The Royal Coat of Arms and much of the original wooden panelling and seating still survive.

Here the Liberty Magistrates met in Petty Sessions and Quarter Sessions, hearing cases and ordering punishments that gradually changed over the years. In early Victorian times those being sentenced could find themselves sent to the nearby prison in St Marygate or transported on a very long journey to Australia. Those going to the Liberty Prison might be serving three months hard labour (usually for theft) which in the 1830s replaced public whippings in the Market Place. Transportation was for persistent offenders. Capital offences - and there were many, despite reform of the penal code - were always referred to the Assizes in York for trial before a judge, as had long been the practice.

Fines as a form of punishment became more common as the 19thC wore on, and by the First World War the motor car was providing a whole new class of fineable offences, as it has continued to do since. The magistrates also had general business to concern them, such as licensing firearms and public houses, swearing in constables and fixing the Poor Rate.

The office of Justice of the Peace goes back to the 14thC, and they were appointed in the Liberty of Ripon as elsewhere from that time onwards. They were there to implement the rules that made an ordered and civilised life possible for the local community, and they played a vital role in the working of the legal system.

In Ripon in the 19thC they were drawn both from the local landed gentry and from the world of commerce and industry (particularly varnish making). The Marquess of Ripon from Studley Royal was Chairman of the Liberty Bench until his death in 1909, whilst other Justices came from such well known families as the Oxleys, the Daltons (Sleningford Park), the Kearsleys, the Williamsons and the Powells (Sharow). Much depended on the advice of a wise Clerk (in the mid-19thC his name *was* Wise!), and for many years the Clerks were provided by the firm of solicitors now known as Hutchinson and Buchanan.

# The Old Deanery

## A Jacobean mansion for the Church

One of Ripon's most important buildings, the Old Deanery in Minster Road stands only a short distance from the spot where the Ripon Jewel was found. Its very location is a reminder that it lies close to the 7thC monastery around which the original Ripon developed, on land which has belonged to the church ever since.

In early medieval times the Archbishop of York had a palace close by, and it was part of his property which was made available in the early 15thC for the construction of a New Bedern on the later Deanery site. Here around a stone quadrangle were built the communal living quarters of the Vicars-Choral who sang the services in the Minster church (this Bedern superseded an earlier one off Bedern Bank).

However, 180 years later, in the closing years of Queen Elizabeth's reign, with the church in Ripon very much in disarray after the Reformation, the new Bedern was clearly much under-used, and it was briefly considered for an ecclesiastical college. Had this happened, it might have developed into a university, but sufficient funding was not available and in 1604 resources instead were put into re-endowing the Collegiate church. A Dean was to head the new Chapter of Canons, and by the 1620s the Bedern buildings had been demolished to make way for an imposing new Deanery, basically the structure that we see today.

The man responsible for this Jacobean mansion (c.1625) appears to have been Miles Moodie, "a man of great learning, honesty and courage", twice Mayor of Ripon and its M.P. briefly in 1645 prior to his death. This was to be the official residence of successive Deans for the next three centuries, and it was built on an imposing scale. Some of its Jacobean panelling still survives, as well as an extremely fine oak staircase which occupies most of the east wing. There have however been several later alterations, particularly in 1799 when a whole range of rooms was added at the rear of the house between the original back projecting wings.

Responsibility for this lay with the then Dean, Robert Darley Waddilove, who had already enjoyed a remarkable church career that included a chaplaincy to the British embassy in Madrid. A scholar and antiquary who also had architectural

interests, he became Dean in 1791 and within a decade had enlarged and enhanced his residence, proudly adding his own initials below the very stylish royal coat of arms that can still be seen over the main door. Earlier (1797) he had embellished the church's very flat west towers with pinnacles and battlements, and in 1809 was to provide the outside clock. Not one to shun publicity, neither was he one to contemplate early retirement, dying in office in 1828 at the age of 92.

Some years later, in 1859, in circumstances as yet unclear, the Deanery's south facade was largely rebuilt with the present mullioned bay windows added. The 20thC brought change of a different kind when in 1941 the newly appointed Dean Birchenough moved out to the nearby Residence (now demolished), so freeing the Deanery for use by the Army for the rest of the war. Since then the 'Old Deanery' has been leased out and run with varying success as a quality restaurant. Now yet another chapter in its history has begun after extensive restoration work at the beginning of the 21stC.

# Thorpe Prebend House

## A new use for an old building

In recent years a very large Lottery grant, with additional funding from English Heritage, has made possible a major refurbishment of Thorpe Prebend House. So why is Thorpe Prebend worth spending so much money on? In Ripon it is a rarity - a Grade II* Jacobean town house with projecting wings, the doors and windows reflecting every century since then. A high status building, it was chosen to provide overnight accommodation for King James I when he visited Ripon in 1617, staying where his mother Mary Queen of Scots may perhaps have been lodged on her brief sojourn in Ripon in 1569.

At that time Thorpe Prebend had passed into private hands, having been confiscated from the church during the Reformation. But for centuries before, the prebendal house of the Canons of Thorpe had stood on the site, and some of the timber work of the medieval structure still survives in the Jacobean rebuild. Perhaps the most interesting of the Canons of Thorpe was the last one - Marmaduke Bradley, who agreed to become Abbot of Fountains in order to help close it down (1539). He then returned to his prebendal house, with a comfortable abbot's pension, only to have the rug pulled from under him when the prebends themselves were dissolved in 1547. Bradley was

ejected, but retired to his last redoubt as Master of the Hospital of St. Mary Magdalen, where he died in 1553.

Thorpe Prebend house passed out of church control into the hands of the Dawson family, and it was George Dawson who substantially rebuilt it in a style fit for a king to enjoy, as actually happened in 1617. Jacobean panelling and a fine fireplace overmantel still survive from that period. From the 1630s onwards the house changed hands many times, and by the 1830s it had been partitioned into 5 separate dwellings.

At the end of the century however Thorpe Prebend found a friend in the Revd John Darnborough, who bought it in order to put it to public use. He died soon after, but his sister knew his wishes and in 1902 set up a group of Trustees to turn it into a public museum. Progress was slow, but in 1912 the Trusteeship was conveyed to Ripon City Council who restored the building and opened it as the City Museum in May 1914. As such it flourished in the interwar years, with a resident caretaker, but in the 1950s growing apathy led to the museum's closure and the dispersal of some of the artefacts.

Although the Friendship Club for the elderly used part of the building in the years that followed, no successful major use was found. Ownership passed to Harrogate Borough Council in 1974 and then back to Ripon City Council in 1990. Ripon Improvement Trust then took it on in 1994 and raised funds for its maintenance, but it was increasingly felt that the natural future of Thorpe Prebend lay where it had begun, with the Church, which had the long-term capacity to maintain the building. Much neglected in the past and now expensively restored, this venerable building will expect much of its new masters.

# The Ripon Ichthyosaurus

### Special protection for ancient bones

When Thorpe Prebend House was the City Museum, from 1914 to the mid-1950s, it contained a very assorted collection of items indeed. Not least impressive

was a pair of geological fossils in sturdy cases mounted high on a wall upstairs, so inaccessible that they became a permanent fixture and even survived the demise of the museum.

The end however finally came on 21st November 2000, when fossil experts Dr. Philip Manning and a colleague from the Yorkshire Museum in York arrived to take the Thorpe Prebend fossils into protective custody. Not without difficulty and with considerable assistance the cases were taken down and the contents despatched to York to be studied and conserved.

The larger of the two specimens was an Ichthyosaurus, about 182 million years old and dating to the early Jurassic period. This strange creature, technically a marine reptile, shared some of the characteristics of the dolphin, the porpoise and the turtle, though the teeth that tore fish and belemnite squids apart most resembled those of a crocodile. This predatory beast also had very large eyes, the better to see its prey in murky waters.

When it died, its heavy head and snout led the way down into the soft sediments of the seabed, and this helped to preserve it from scavengers. In the case of the Thorpe Prebend example the snout and body (encrusted with ammonites) have survived well but three of the flippers and the tail have been lost. The other fossil was a Lepidotus fish of the same period, a much smaller sea creature that had heavy scales and crushing teeth. The geologists were pleased that its head was unusually intact.

Millions of years after their deaths, vast geological upheavals raised up the ancient seabed and turned it into cliffs, exposing its buried contents. Both the fossils came from the Whitby area and were among the many that were found during alum mining in the late 19thC.

In 1882 the Ripon Naturalists' Club and Scientific Association was set up, and premises were acquired in Park Street that later became Ripon's first museum. Various private collections of natural history items were soon donated, including the large collection of Mr. Charles William Rothery of Littlethorpe Hall, presented by the trustees of his estate. According to an 1885 description of this collection – valued at £14,000 at the time of its bequest – "the fossils are numerous, and there are 2 or 3 ichthysauri [sic], splendid specimens, and the ganoid fishes and ammomets are in great variety".

In August 1896 Ripon Corporation was invited by the Naturalists' Club to take over its collection of birds, animals and geological specimens. The Corporation put the collection into its Park Street museum, only to remove it later to the Town Hall when the Spa Baths were built and the museum demolished... The collections were finally put on display in Thorpe Prebend when the City Museum opened there in 1914. Certainly whoever fastened the fossil cases to the wall intended them to stay there for a long time!

# Ripon Grammar School

## From High St. Agnesgate to Bishopton Close

The future of the Grammar School has hung in the balance on several occasions in its history, and one such period of uncertainty came in the 1870s. Until then Ripon boys were able to have an education in Greek and Latin free of charge in the school which then lay on the north side of High St. Agnesgate where the Cathedral Hall now stands. The main classroom was arranged with pupils' desks along the walls with one master on his 'throne' halfway down the room and another at the end.

Earlier in the 19thC the school had been doing well under a number of scholarly headmasters but in 1868 the number of boys on the roll had shrunk to 22 from the 50-60 of former times. One reason for this was the curriculum. Whilst the exclusive teaching of classical subjects had been broken to a certain extent, no science was taught and for other non-classical subjects such as arithmetic a fee was often charged. The curriculum was more suited to those preparing for one of the learned professions, and few Ripon parents aspired to this for their sons. The schoolmaster of the day suggested that the limit of 15 on the number of boarders (whose fees augmented his income) was at fault for the declining reputation of the school.

However the restricted nature of the site meant that it would be difficult to provide the facilities increasingly required for a reputable school at that time - and the condition of the premises could not have helped. They were described in a report of c.1870 to the Charity Commission as disgraceful, the conveniences being in a "disgusting and abominable" state. Hardly better were the classrooms, where the floors were so rotten that "the boys amuse themselves by sowing peas in the soil beneath the seats".

But realisation of the reduced prestige of the school, coupled with national legislation that encouraged such schools to broaden their curriculum or accept a lower status, meant that change was coming. A programme of reform was accepted by the governors but there were still considerable problems.

Local people, who had at first reacted enthusiastically to the news of reform, began a campaign against the measures when they realised that their 'free' Grammar School would go. It was however eventually agreed that the fees would not be as high as had originally been thought and that the governors would have the power to reduce or forego them for a limited number of poor pupils.

Just when it was realised that the

school's ancient endowments were not sufficient to provide the new premises which the reforms required, the school was able to benefit from the misfortune of others. In 1874 the headmaster of a private school at Bishopton, to the west of the city, died and his school had to close. Lord Ripon, who owned the freehold of the premises, immediately offered them to the Grammar School free of charge, together with a capital sum to purchase further land. The offer was accepted, and so Ripon Grammar School was able to move out of its cramped and insanitary premises to a new site with space for laboratories, a gymnasium and pitches for cricket and rugby. A whole new era of expansion lay ahead.

# Jepson's Hospital

## The Bluecoat School

The familiar red brick building on Water Skellgate, now Ripon City Club, began life in the late 19thC as a school, replacing an even earlier school building that resembled a pair of cottages. This was Jepson's Hospital, commonly known in the town as the Bluecoat School from the uniform worn by its pupils - blue suit, cap and stockings plus a cape lined with yellow.

The school had been founded through a bequest by Zacharias Jepson, an apothecary who died in 1672 at the age of 49. Like Ripon's almshouses it was a 'hospital' in the old sense of being a charitable establishment to help the needy - in this case poor children. Jepson left his house and £3000 to provide a place where 20 local orphan boys and the sons of poor tradesmen could receive not just free education but board and lodging too. In addition they were to be helped to become apprentices, or even to go on to university (in cases approved by the Master of the Grammar School). Jepson intended a close link between his school and the Grammar School, and made the curious stipulation that the Usher (Second Master) of the Free Grammar School was to be the Master of the Hospital - provided that he was a Bachelor of Arts (which was not always the case).

Obviously a practical man, Jepson also provided in his will for the boys' clothes to be washed and mended - by 'a poor freeman's widow' - who would also do the cleaning. The boys (aged at least 7) were selected by Feoffees (Trustees) who on the two days of the year that they met were to enjoy the use of two silver tankards and two silver beer cups, a special legacy for the purpose. Jepson's widow Isobel however had clearly not been consulted about these terms

since she contested the will and succeeded in reducing the capital bequest - which in turn lowered the number of boys from 20 to 12. No doubt to the chagrin of the Feoffees the widow also kept back one each of the silver tankards and beer cups.

Two centuries later the school was still in the same premises and it still provided free boarding education for poor Ripon boys, though numbers had fluctuated. Only seven pupils had gone on to university, but the school had enjoyed more success in helping the boys to obtain apprenticeships. It had been a long time since the Master of Jepson's Hospital had been a Grammar School Usher - perhaps partly for this reason he had also taken fee-paying pupils to augment his income, some of them being the sons of 'respectable Ripon tradesmen'.

By the 1870s, despite a number of further bequests, the school was in financial difficulties just at a time when the premises were in such bad condition that they needed to be rebuilt. A public appeal was made to try to raise the funding, but in 1878 the Feoffees went ahead regardless with the new building which opened in 1880, though the full cost was not covered until 1892.

Despite having fee-paying boarders the school was still in difficulties, and in 1927 the Board of Education decided that a charity school of this type was no longer necessary. The Master and remaining pupils were transferred to the Grammar School and the property was sold to Messrs. T. & R. Williamson, varnish manufacturers, who sold on the buildings to their present owners, the City Club. The endowments of the Bluecoat School were directed to more general educational needs in the town (the details are recorded on a board in the Town Hall corridor), but inevitably there were many who sadly regretted the demise of an ancient local institution.

# The Workhouse

### An institution unfairly maligned?

The complex of buildings off Allhallowgate known as Sharow View contains Ripon's Poor Law museum, appropriately housed in what was once part of the Workhouse - a salutary reminder that Ripon has had its share of social problems in the past.

An attitude of sympathy and concern towards those most in need was slow to develop over the centuries; in the late Middle Ages and early Tudor times there was much hostility towards those with no work, especially beggars, and many suffered the stocks or worse. But there were also orphans, the disabled and the elderly infirm, and for them there was only private charity and the parish poor-box (Ripon was fortunate to have three sets of almshouses).

In the 16thC, however, it was increasingly accepted in government circles that private generosity was not sufficient, and that the only answer was for a compulsory Poor Rate, levied on all householders. It was to be dispensed by unpaid Overseers of the Poor, appointed by magistrates. Pauper children were to be apprenticed, and the aged and infirm would receive grants of food and clothes in their homes, but the able-bodied unemployed were still viewed with profound suspicion and often sent to Houses of Correction to learn the virtues of honest toil. By 1686 Ripon had its own House of Correction in St. Marygate.

The parish relief system, set up by the great Elizabethan statutes of 1598 and 1601, survived into the early 19thC and for much of that time seems to have worked well. Those most in need received relief in cash or clothing, had medical bills paid for them and even had ale and tobacco provided. Many parishes owned cottages (Town Houses) which were let cheaply to the poor, but paupers deemed to be the responsibility of another parish and unable to provide the necessary settlement papers were unceremoniously moved on. Those of all ages incapable of coping on their own finished up in the town Poor House.

The economic disruption of the early 19thC led to the Poor Law system being drastically changed by the Act of 1834, the reaction to an enormous increase in the Poor Rate, especially in distressed industrial areas. Parliament decided that there was far too much 'outdoor relief' and it had to be stopped. Those in need would have to enter the Workhouse - more would be built, and they would be

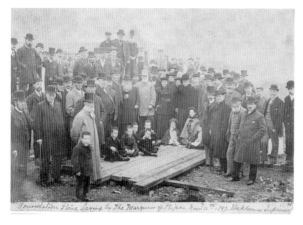

Foundation Stone Laying by The Marquess of Ripon Nov 11th 1847, Mr Kerrans Superior

properly run by elected Boards of Guardians under central government scrutiny. There were delays in implementing the act, partly because of objections, and Ripon's workhouse was not built until 1854 (on the site of the former Poor House). The majority of the inmates were the sick, the elderly, the mentally ill and parentless children, though after 1877 there was special provision for vagrants, who were given overnight accommodation in a new Casual Ward, with 15 cells and a Dayroom.

How unpleasant was life in Ripon's Victorian workhouse? It was a strictly regulated community run to provide only basic services, but in later years special treats became common, like the "usual fare of roast beef and plum pudding" at Christmas (1900), followed by the Mayor's tea and entertainment. In 1907 the Mayor's entertainment included marionettes, Punch and Judy, a pianoforte duet, two violin cello solos, and a recitation whose "witticisms kept the audience in roars of laughter". Certainly if you spurned luxury, had limited needs, disliked loneliness and enjoyed company, the Workhouse had something to offer.

# The House of Correction

### Rogues, vagabonds and sturdy beggars

It still comes as a surprise for some to learn that the curious redbrick building with barred windows in St. Marygate was once a well-equipped Victorian prison serving the needs of the Liberty of Ripon. The prison's origins go back to the 17thC when Houses of Correction were being set up nationally to tackle the problems of vagrancy and unemployment. The stern attitude of those times decreed that in those institutions "rogues, vagabonds, sturdy beggars and disorderly persons" be set to work on raw materials and so reformed out of their idle ways.

In 1629 Ripon Corporation asked the Archbishop of York to provide a House of Correction in the town, but it was to be another 57 years and a Civil War later before such provision was finally made (1686), this time on the initiative of local magistrates. This building still survives, with its fine rows of mullioned windows in St Marygate looking towards the Cathedral, providing the street with its most distinctive architectural feature.

The house was built on land belonging to the Dean and Chapter, and the Liberty magistrates negotiated one lease after another with the church authorities over the next two centuries. The first Master was appointed in 1686 and for much of the 18thC the salary was £15 a year; in the 1770s the remuneration was actually reduced, and the then Master Michael Gregg left (1778) to take over the Sign of the *Minster* which he doubtless found to be more remunerative. Punishing offenders remained the prime function of the House of Correction in the 18thC; for example in 1768 Thomas Iveson was committed there for ten days "to be whipped and kept to hard labour" for burning the Ling Heath and Furze on Bishopside Moor.

By Napoleonic times the Liberty magistrates deemed a substantial enlargement of the building to be necessary, and it was decided to build a whole new prison block on the north side of the original House of Correction, which then became the Governor's private residence. The work was completed in 1816. As part of a wider reorganisation, the Liberty Gaol (now the Old Curiosity Shop) near the Cathedral was demoted to a debtors' prison and all other categories of prisoners were transferred to St. Marygate.

A very full picture of life in a small early Victorian prison is revealed by the records of the 1840s. 40 to 50 offenders passed through its cells each year with an average of five incarcerated at any one time. These were petty offenders rarely serving more than three month sentences and often less than two weeks. The prison was mixed, but the majority of inmates were male, mostly aged 17 to 30 and convicted for theft or under the Vagrancy, Game and Bastardy laws. In these early years those sentenced to hard labour suffered the rigours of the Treadwheel. The diet consisted of carefully measured portions of bread, meat, potatoes, soup and oatmeal gruel. However, by the 1860s the emphasis was on reform and there was a matron, surgeon, barber and chaplain to attend the inmates. There was even a library and sick bay.

In 1878 Ripon's House of Correction and Liberty Gaol finally closed as part of a Government purge of small prisons. However, within ten years it had become the Police Station for the County Constabulary and was to remain as such until a more modern building was provided in 1956. After years of uncertainty the cellblock was put to a very appropriate use in the early 1980s as a Prison and Police Museum, and it has been steadily enlarged and improved over the years since.

# The Theatre

## A victim of changing taste

Those who have been mightily impressed by Richmond's Georgian theatre will be saddened to learn that there was once a similar one in Ripon which failed to survive the years. However, some details about it have come down to us.

It was located in Park Street, on the corner with Firby Lane, where a bus depot stood not many years ago. In Napoleonic times, genteel society in the town could choose the theatre as an alternative to the Races and the Assembly Rooms for their entertainment and recreation, and patrons from Studley Royal would find the theatre conveniently sited on their approach road to Ripon.

As at Richmond, the theatre came complete with Pit, Boxes and Gallery, and was favoured by Samuel Butler's famous troupe of players, *His Majesty's Servants*, whose circuit included Richmond, Northallerton, Harrogate, Beverley and Whitby. Briefly (c.1808) among their number was the young Edmund Kean, who went on to become the great Shakespearean heart-throb of his day. Kean was renowned for his expressive eyes - this sketch was actually found in a Ripon collection and is probably contemporary.

There is uncertainty regarding both the origins and the demise of the theatre. It appears to have first opened its doors on 20 August 1792, but Butler's players had performed in Ripon before this in some other premises. George Hassell, one time Recorder of the Borough, is credited with building the theatre, but he had died in 1778 and was therefore probably associated with the earlier building. Perhaps it was his son, also George Hassell, who signed the lease in 1792 agreeing to provide both site and new theatre, but in the process causing later confusion.

According to a contemporary description of the theatre, "the scenery and decorations are excellent, and the manager endeavours to provide a respectable

dramatic corps, with the novelties of the day, for the gratification of the public during the seasin". The theatre had seating for some 320 people, and despite being lit by candles was never burnt down. Butler's company numbered about a dozen and had a repertoire of a hundred plays. An evening's entertainment was varied to say the least - the playbill shown (1800) advertises the (alleged) London success *The Castle Spectre*, and the special effects on offer included sliding panels, a subterraneous Dungeon, and 'transparencies'. This was followed by songs (*The Bonny Bold Soldier* and *Sally in our Alley)*, and then a farce, *High Life below Stairs*. A playbill on a later occasion promised that "A

Splendid Balloon (weather permitting) will ascend outside the Theatre, at half-past six precisely, to announce the Opening of the Doors".

The problem dating the demise of the theatre stems from the fact that although by the late 1830s the building had become a Riding School, and later a Drill Hall, play bills survive for 1839 and even 1849. By then the Public Rooms had opened in Water Skellgate (enlarged in the 1880s to become the Victoria Hall) and this was probably the new performance venue. However in the early 1850s a new Theatre Royal opened in Blossomgate with a performance of *William Tell* by the Ripon Amateur Dramatic Society; *Pizarro*, *Macbeth* and the pantomime *St. Wilfrid in the Olden Time* followed, catering for all tastes. But this theatre too did not last long, falling victim either to changing taste or competition from the Public Rooms.

# Cinemas

## The Golden Oldies

Although Ripon had a theatre from the late 18thC, there was no major centre for popular entertainment until the Public Rooms were opened in 1834 in Water Skellgate, on the corner with Low Skellgate. Even this was seen as inadequate in later Victorian times, and in 1885 the Ripon Public Rooms Company raised money "to erect a large hall suitable for holding public meetings, performance of stage plays, and any other public purpose required". The money was raised (nearly £3000) and the Public Rooms were replaced by the ambitious Victoria Hall, capable of housing 1000 persons.

Over the next twenty years the Hall was used for a variety of purposes, including exhibitions, bazaars, gymnastic displays and even a Ball held to celebrate

the relief of Mafeking (1900). In 1908, after extensive renovation, it was re-named the Victoria Opera House, and the following year 'The Gondoliers' was performed there by Ripon Operatic Society. In 1910 Ripon Orchestral Society gave its first concert there.

At this time, however, new technology had arrived in the form of the moving picture, and by 1914 the Victoria Opera House, now styled the 'Electric Theatre', had began to be used for cinema shows. It was owned by the Campbell Cinematograph Company who found a mass audience on their doorstep from 1915-19 in the form of soldiers at Ripon's new Army Camp. Doubtless they came in droves to sample the delights of silent films with piano accompaniment.

Other uses of the building continued, however, including stage plays, children's events, whist drives, and - in the Roaring Twenties - ballroom dancing. Management changes followed, and in 1930 the Talkies arrived, but the opening film *Broadway Melody*, to which the Corporation had been invited, was marred by a technical fault - the electricity supply failed. An electrical fault (and not a bomb) was no doubt to blame too for the serious fire which burnt out most of the interior of the building in 1943, but it reopened with new seating in less than twelve months.

By the 1960s wrestling matches were being presented there, along with operatic performances and bingo. But the cinema was on the way out, and in August 1967 the last film was shown.

Since March 1916 however, film-goers in Ripon had had an alternative venue to frequent - the Palladium in Kirkgate, where shows were provided nightly with matinees on Thursdays and Saturdays. Prices were 3d., 6d., and 1 shilling (children half price), but they rose with the arrival of talkies in 1930! The cinema's best years then came and went, and terminal decline set in as public tastes

changed. Final closure came in 1982.

It seems that a third Ripon cinema - the New Spa Cinema in Park Street - existed briefly in the period 1919 - 22. It stood opposite the Spa Hotel (near the present tennis courts), but did not long survive the closure of the army camp.

# Ripon Spa

## A rival to Harrogate?

The grand entrance to the swimming baths in Park Street is a familiar enough sight, but it is easy to forget that its imposing facade relates to a rather different use - an attempt to establish Ripon in the Edwardian world of international spas, and so cash in on some of the pecuniary benefits then being enjoyed by fashionable Harrogate. Concern to attract visitors to Ripon is nothing new.

Ripon's immediate problem was that it lacked the necessary medicinal waters, but this was seen as no obstacle by the enterprising Marquess of Ripon, one

of the main promoters of the scheme, who arranged for appropriate spring water from Aldfield to be piped across his Fountains/Studley estate down to Ripon.

An Edwardian Spa however required not just medicinal water but all the extras too - a high quality Spa Hotel where wealthy visitors could stay, Spa Gardens where they could take the air, meet their friends, and perhaps listen to the band on a sunny day. By 1909, when the Marquess died, all these facilities were in place, soon to be joined in the Spa Gardens by his own imposing statue.

H.R.H. PRINCESS VICTORIA EUGENIE.
*Photo by Hughes & Mullins.*

The new Spa offered immersion baths including the latest electrical treatment (!) as well as glasses of sulphur water, a 'mild aperient', at 1d. a time. Gout was among the upper class complaints thought to benefit from this regime.

The prime event of this whole episode had been the formal opening of the Spa Baths (using a solid gold key) on the 24 October 1905 by Princess Henry of Battenberg and Princess Victoria Eugenie ('Ena'), seen here arriving

in front of a guard of honour provided by the West Yorkshire Regiment, backed by curious onlookers. Hopefully the royal princesses were impressed by the yellow terracotta finish to the carriage porch and ornate pump room, designed by Samuel Stead, and still striking today. Later the same day they went on to open a Schools' Bazaar in the Victoria Hall in Water Skellgate.

'Princess Henry' was in fact Beatrice, youngest daughter of Queen Victoria, and widowed since Prince Henry of Battenberg's death in 1896. 'Ena' was their only daughter, and it was actually her 18th birthday on the day of her visit to Ripon. Within a year she had married King Alphonso XIII of Spain, and went on to have 7 children in 7 years. King Juan Carlos is her grandson.

The Ripon Spa was never a great success; perhaps it came too late to the spa scene, or was upstaged by Harrogate. A serious fire in April 1917 was a major setback, and after the First World War public tastes steadily changed. By the early 1930s demand for a swimming bath greatly exceeded support for the Spa, and in 1936 the building was duly converted to that use. Since then it has provided an excellent service to the people of Ripon, but the discerning observer in the foyer will still sense traces of its Edwardian grandeur.


# The Gazebo

### Genteel pleasures in the Age of Elegance

Ripon is fortunate in having an excellent example of a sophisticated garden feature of the 18thC known as a Gazebo - and like the Obelisk, there is only the one example in town.

What was a Gazebo? The word is mock Latin, and was used to describe a small tower or pavilion set in the corner of a large garden to enable Georgian gentry to have their cake and eat it - to enjoy the privacy of a walled garden whilst still being able to look out beyond it and admire distant views - or more likely perhaps to idle their time sipping drinks while gossiping with friends and discussing passers-by.

In Ripon's case, the gazebo was a grand affair, consisting of not one but two pavilions, linked by a balustraded promenade, although a map of 1800 perhaps in error shows the two pavilions with no linking terrace. Built almost certainly in the early 18thC, this ornate feature lies at the far end of the garden of the large house now known as 7-8 Park Street, now a doctors' surgery. In this position, in addition to overlooking Church Lane, it would have offered fine rural prospects to the north and west of the town, as well as glimpses of the Minster and the Obelisk to the east. The property itself stood in what was the fashionable quarter of the town in those days, close to the new Georgian theatre (by the 1790s) and not far from the Assembly Rooms (1800).

This large composite gazebo (also called by contemporaries a Cupola) is not surprisingly a Grade II* Listed building. Constructed of brick with stone edgings, the 2-storey pavilions have pyramid-shaped pantile roofs. Between them lies the balustraded raised walkway, adorned with four large round-headed niches. Beneath the gallery are arched tunnels where garden equipment could be stored.

The history of the Gazebo has yet to be fully explored but it seems most probable that its creator was Roger Bayne, described as a 'gentleman' and certainly a man of substance who left money to the poor on his death in 1719. His son Richard Bayne inherited the family wealth and property - trained in the law, he was to hold the post of Recorder of Ripon for 44 years. By the end of the 18thC however the house with its fashionable extravaganza had changed hands several times, and at some stage between 1800 and 1833 the garden was divided lengthwise by the brick wall visible in the photograph, no doubt reflecting major alterations to the house itself. The division of the property, including the Gazebo, may well have marked the onset of the latter's deterioration, which was very evident by the middle of the 20thC when the whole structure was in danger of collapse.

Vigorous campaigning by various local groups, especially the Civic Society, eventually led in 1986 to the restoration of the eastern half of the Gazebo which was in the ownership of Harrogate Borough Council. Since then restoration work has also taken place to the western half which was in private ownership, as a result of which this rare and grandiose structure has been given a new lease of life. Access remains restricted, but the rear of the gazebo can readily be viewed from Spa Park.

# The Clock Tower

### Marking the passing of time

Enthusiasm for festivals comes and goes, but in recent years they have become very much in vogue in Ripon. A similar period of enthusiasm seems to have been triggered over a century ago by the great Millenary Festival of 1886 which was

THE OPENING OF THE CLOCK TOWER,
CORONATION DAY, 1898.

soon followed by a series of attempted sequels. Sandwiched somewhere near the middle of all this festivity was a great national - even international - event: Queen Victoria's Diamond Jubilee in 1897 which celebrated 'Sixty Glorious Years'.

Ripon inevitably saw this as an opportunity not to be missed, and addressed the challenge of devising appropriate events. Mayor Tom Williamson arranged (not without dissent) for twelve lime trees to be planted in February around the Market Place by twelve former mayors, Jubilee medals (do any survive?) were presented to schoolchildren, there was a Yorkshire tea for Sunday School children, and a free dinner for the Over-Sixties in June. There were bonfires and fireworks, a special Cathedral service, and a civic luncheon to record the official presentation of the Town Hall to the City by the Marquess of Ripon.

There was also a brand new building to celebrate - the Victoria Clock Tower at the end of Palace Road. In June 1897 the Corporation agreed that this privately-funded scheme should go ahead, and a year later on 28th June 1898 the key was handed over to the Mayor before a large crowd at a ceremony which involved a galaxy of dignitaries. The City Band played the National Anthem and the sun shone on the proceedings. Speakers expressed loyal sentiments towards the Queen, and the Bishop won a laugh by suggesting the Tower had been built at the Cross-roads of Ripon (it had been paid for by the Cross sisters, Misses Frances Mary and Constance Cross of Coney Garths, next to Holy Trinity Church). Predictably the day ended with a tea party.

The Tower was designed by George Corson, a Leeds architect. Its apex is appropriately designed in the shape of a crown with pinnacles at the base of each

of the eight curved ribs and a small metal crown at the very top. In a canopied niche on a corbel sits the statue of Queen Victoria, gazing serenely towards the town, while beneath her is the small doorway which allowed access for the clock-winder. The 8-day clock is by Potts & Sons of Leeds, and every effort was made over the years to maintain its accuracy and avoid causing unnecessary alarm to those hurrying along North Road to catch a train. The downstairs room was for no other use, and there has never been confirmation of the rumour over the years that milk-bottles have been seen on the door step.

In 1953 Ripon's Highway Committee discussed moving the Clock Tower in order to alleviate traffic problems at the road junction, but the idea was dropped when 300 people signed a petition opposing it, and the Tower has stood its ground ever since, despite the proposal of further radical solutions in the 1990s. The introduction of traffic lights proved to be a simple but effective answer, and the Queen's monument, a Grade II Listed Building, remains in its original setting, finely refurbished in 2003.

# The Canal

### 'Ripon: By Divine Foresight a Harbour'

A visit to the Canal Basin in Bondgate is a reminder of the great improvements that have taken place to Ripon's Canal since the mid 1980s, transforming it from a state of dereliction into one of the city's most attractive assets. The Canal has certainly had its good and bad times. It all began in the upbeat days of the 1760s when a confident Ripon Corporation took the view that the town would benefit greatly from a canal - and this at a time when canals were still a comparative novelty. By establishing a connection to the Ure at a point where it was navigable, Ripon would be able to enjoy all the benefits of water links to York, Hull and the coalfields of south Yorkshire. Nature had bestowed on the town a favourable location: *Ripon - by Divine Foresight a Harbour* was to be the proud boast of the Navigation's logo.

In September 1766 Mayor Braithwaite convened a meeting at the *York Minster Inn* (now Boots) to test support for the project and begin the process of securing the necessary Act of Parliament. The 42-year-old engineer John Smeaton, builder of the Eddystone lighthouse, was invited to draw up the technical plans and related costings, and these were accepted at a subsequent meeting in October, this time at the *Royal Oak* in Kirkgate. The Bill received the Royal Assent in April 1767.

Building work began that same year, much of it under the direction of Smeaton's assistant William Jessop, with final responsibility lying with the Ure Navigation Commissioners. Much of the

stone for the locks appears to have come from quarries at Burton Leonard and South Stainley, and the water supply came of course from the Skell via a subterranean conduit. Other engineering works along the Ure had to be completed and the project went well over budget, but from 1773 the Canal was open, tolls were being levied, and barges were delivering goods - sand, gravel, agricultural produce and particularly coal.

It seems however that those who had invested in the scheme were to be disappointed, since running costs and maintenance absorbed nearly all the revenue. By 1820 substantial arrears of interest payments were owed and the Commissioners were in trouble. Parliament intervened to set up a new Company to run the Ure Navigation. More capital was raised and various improvements carried out, but a problem was looming beyond the Company's control. The railways were coming, and in 1846 the Directors of the Leeds-Thirsk Railway Company were authorised to take ownership of the Ure Navigation Company. Once the Ripon line had officially opened in 1848 the canal business went into steady decline, the coal trade being particularly affected by the new fierce competition. Maintenance inevitably suffered and by the First World War the canal was virtually devoid of commerce (though busy with skaters during cold winters).

The founding of the Ripon Motor Boat Club in 1931 and the advent of pleasure craft kept Oxclose lock in operation, to preserve access to the Ure, but by the late 1930s the upper locks were closed and padlocked. Worse followed in the 1950s when these locks were demolished. However by the 1980s times had changed dramatically; the expanding pleasure craft industry had created a new market force which by stages was to bring Ripon's canal and its basin back into full use, an ongoing process enhanced in 2002 by the opening of a large and impressive marina.

# The Racecourse

### A long pedigree

Ripon is known nationally in the world of horse racing, and it was not a late arrival on that scene. As with much else in the city (e.g. the Army, the Grammar School), the connection goes back centuries.

Horse-racing began to take off in the pleasure-seeking days of the late 17thC, when King Charles II himself was a patron of the Turf, and the support of the local gentry helped to get Ripon involved in the new sport. Although there are references to horses being raced on Bondgate Green in the 1660s, the first official race course (of four miles) was set up by the Corporation in 1714 on High Common (where the Golf Club now is), and it was to continue there for over a hundred years.

One of the most important early supporters of Ripon's races was undoubtedly the celebrated John Aislabie, who turned his attention to more local matters after the South Sea Bubble disaster, and patronised the races with annual gifts of prize money from 1722 to 1724. In 1723 his

A bronze Medallion struck in 1865 to commemorate the erection of the Old Ripon Racecourse Grandstand, now S. Olave's School. It admitted the subscriber for seven years.

wife Judith gave a silver teapot and canister to be run for by gentlewomen (was this a first for Ripon?). We are told that nine women "mounted their steeds, rid astride, were dressed in drawers, waistcoats and jockey caps, their shapes transparent, and a vast concourse of people to see them" as they competed for the Lady's Plate.

Racing continued on the High Common for over a hundred years until it was ended by the enclosure of the Common in 1826. However, a replacement site was eventually found in 1837, this time across the river on the north bank of the Ure. Mr Matthew Haygarth – appropriately the publican of the *Horse and Jockey* - led the way by making his own fields available, and eventually a stand was built and races held there annually, soon benefiting no doubt from the proximity of the Railway Station (1848).

Even so, there was a problem - probably it was the racecourse's location on the flood plain of the Ure which led to it being relocated to higher ground, at Red Bank, this time overlooking the valley of the Skell. In February 1865 the foundation stone of the new grandstand was laid by the Mayor, and in 1880 Ripon Race Company was formed to purchase the grandstand from the former Race Committee. Capital was raised through the sale of shares and two race meetings were held a year. Part of this grandstand has survived, incorporated into the Cathedral Choir School.

Even this site however was eventually thought not good enough. At the very end of the century (1899) a new Ripon Race Company was formed and the present course opened, on the eastern edge of the town, and once again near the Ure. The first meeting was held there in August 1900 when a large crowd packed into the new grandstand to see the

Great St Wilfrid Handicap and other races. The new course flourished and was used for other purposes - rare archive film of April 1916 shows soldiers from the Army Camp enjoying their sports day there, and later the Royal Flying Corps had aeroplanes based there. In the years following the Great War, the Racecourse has been enhanced in many ways and extra facilities provided. Its grounds are beautifully maintained and it deserves recognition as one of the city's major attractions.

# The Railway

## When the trains first came to Ripon
The idea of bringing trains to Ripon on a Leeds-Thirsk line originated in the early 1840s during the period of 'Railway Mania' and was part of a grand scheme to improve transport links between the industrial West Riding and the North-East - at the same time of course benefiting the people of Harrogate and Ripon. At Thirsk there would be access to the existing track from York to Darlington (a direct line to Northallerton was soon to provide an alternative route).

After the act had passed Parliament in 1845, construction work soon began and by March 1847 the action had reached Ripon, when the first pile for the railway viaduct was driven into the bed of the Ure. The Cathedral bells were rung, and there was 'much rejoicing'. Other work soon followed - the raising of embankments, the building of bridges and abutments, the laying of track - and an army of navvies descended on the town.

In May1848 progress on the railway was publicised by sending free of charge the first trainload of passengers (plus a navvies' band!) from Ripon to Thirsk and back, a novel experience indeed, and by September the Ripon-Harrogate stretch too was open. The railway brought permanent jobs - station master, clerks, porters, platelayers, etc. - and also important visitors, not least Queen Victoria herself in September 1858 when the royal train stopped in Ripon to take on water and the forewarned City Fathers were able to slip a Loyal Address through the carriage window.

Many other VIPs came to Ripon in the ensuing years including Edward Prince of Wales in 1863, William Gladstone in 1887 and George Prince of Wales in 1904, usually heading for the Marquess's mansion at Studley Royal. Less distinguished visitors could travel from the Station to the Market Place by courtesy of the *Unicorn*'s horse-drawn omnibus, motorised in Edwardian times. During the First World War troops arrived in Ripon by train in their thousands, often marching through the town centre en route to the Army Camp. Inevitably there were occasional railway accidents, as in July 1919 when Herbert Grayson, a shunter, was crushed whilst coupling up trucks at Littlethorpe.

By then the Leeds and Thirsk Railway Company had long since disappeared, changing to the Leeds Northern Railway in 1851 and then merging with others to form the very successful North Eastern Railway Company in 1854. Years later, in 1923, the Ripon line became part of the L.N.E.R. Company, and later still British Railways.

However, by the early 1960s questions were being raised about the economic viability of the line, but attempts to mobilise public opinion in favour of its retention met with an apathetic response. There was little resistance to the eventual decision to end passenger services in March 1967 and goods services in October 1969. Since then much of the railway trackbed has been used for the Bypass, and parts of the line have been built on. Could an acceptable corridor still be found for a restored railway? Time will tell.

# The Water and Sewage Works

## The sweet smell of success

The major improvements that have taken place in Ripon since the mid-1990s are a reminder that the Victorian period too was an Age of Improvement, and at that time they were working from a much lower base. Nowhere was that more true than in the field of Public Health, where the state of the drinking water and the disposal of raw sewage were matters of life and death.

For centuries Ripon's drinking water had come from rainwater, wells and the rivers Skell and Laver. It was sold from leather bags borne by horses, as was still the case until the late 18thC when Alderman William Askwith also arranged for it to be pumped up Duck Hill by the mill wheel that stood at the foot of the bank. The water, which came from the Laver dam at High Cleugh, was then distributed, if intermittently, in pipes around the town.

Whatever the state of the water in the millrace, that of the Skell was undoubtedly contaminated, and an alarming outbreak of cholera in 1854 fuelled demand from the fast growing population for a reliable supply of clean drinking water. In 1864 Ripon Corporation offered a prize of 50 guineas for the best scheme to supply the city adequately.

As many as 23 schemes were submitted, some favouring the pumping of water from the Ure, others favouring a gravitational supply from high ground to the west of the town. The winner (chosen by the City Engineer of Leeds) was a pumping scheme devised by Messrs. Stevenson and Utley of Halifax by which water was to be taken from the Ure above North Bridge, filtered and then pumped by steam power up to a summit reservoir on Lark Hill, from which it would flow by gravity

into the mains. Work proceeded apace, and the new Waterworks, costing nearly £6000, was formally opened by the Mayor in November 1865.

However, it proved to be a mistake. The Ure water was poorly filtered and consequently often muddy until special filter beds were added late in the 1870s. But the main problem, which surprisingly was not anticipated, was the flooding of the riverside pumping station. By the later 1870s there was growing public anger, and in a referendum held in 1877 ratepayers voted two-to-one in favour of a gravitation supply. Even then nothing happened until the great flood of 1883 when the valves of the pumps were choked with silt and supply to the city was entirely cut off. At last there was action, and the outcome was the construction of the Lumley Moor reservoir on land mostly belonging to the ever-helpful Marquess. The new waterworks was opened in 1888, Ripon's second within 23 years.

Within ten years an equally important public health amenity had also appeared - the new sewage works at Fishergreen. Opened by the Marquess himself, then Mayor, in October 1896, it was the logical finale to the proliferation of sewage pipes that followed the general adoption of the water closet, an ingenious device which marked the beginning of the end for dunghills, earth-closets, cess-pits and stenches, and brought relief to the whole country. The Mayor and Corporation had every reason to look proud, if also a little self-satisfied, as they enjoyed the sweet smell of success.

## Skittergate Gutter and Princess Road

### From stinking ditch to local beauty spot

One of the most popular watering-holes on the route of St. Wilfrid's summer procession is undoubtedly the *Magdalens* pub, at the corner of Stonebridgegate and Princess Road. It takes its name from the nearby Hospital of St. Mary Magdalen whose Leper Chapel dates back to the 12thC, but the pub itself needless to say is much more recent.

However, Stonebridgegate is an ancient highway recorded from early medieval times - it was the street or road that led to the stone bridge across the Ure, constructed by the 13thC to give the new Market Place traders an all-weather route to the north, thereby replacing the earlier seasonal ford a little way downstream. By the 19thC the road was also known as Stammergate.

An important feature of this area, running roughly on the line of present day

Princess Road, was a natural water-course which originated on high ground above North Road and flowed eastwards down the gentle slope towards and under Stonebridgegate, eventually running into the Ure at a point where a modern drainage pipe in the river bank still marks the original outflow.

Natural water courses tended to be abused, and this one was no exception. It was known as Skittergate Gutter (the derivation obvious) and it was a stinking open sewer, as was graphically pointed out in 1873 by the then Medical Officer of Health, Dr Thomas Collier, in his reports to Ripon Corporation. At a time when there were regular cases of typhoid and gastric fever in the area, Dr. Collier described Skittergate Gutter in these terms: "at the bottom of Stonebridgegate, is an open ditch, ill-constructed with many angles and turns, sometimes almost stagnant, with filth in it that must have been there for a long time, showing on its half-dried surface evidence of bubbles containing sewer gas. This ditch carries away the sewage from rather more than half the city......." He went on to refer to the foul smells to which those living in the yards and slums of Stonebridgegate were subjected, and concluded by stating that "Skittergate Gutter is simply a disgrace to any town".

By the early 1870s, therefore, the sanitary problems of this part of town were being well-publicised and with surprisingly quick results, no doubt hastened by the needs of the new terraced housing in Princess Road, publicly opened in 1875. By the early 1880s the Medical Officer could report major sanitary improvements, and no doubt among these was the covering over of Skittergate Gutter - soon to be forgotten until years later when householders in Princess Road found that their subsidence problems were caused as much by an ancient watercourse as by gypsum deposits.

The *'Mags'* was part of the Princess Road development of the early 1870s, and although it was sited surprisingly close to the notorious Gutter, new drainage soon turned the situation round - in 1901, when Joseph Wright's pub was checked by the magistrates in their survey, they gave it a good report and declared there to be no sanitary defects. (The report also mentioned that it had a stand-up bar, 2 bedrooms for visitors and stabling for three horses).

The *Magdalens* has retained its character and popularity over the years, improvements have continued, and nowadays this corner of Ripon, looking out over Paddy's Park with the slums long gone, is one of the city's beauty spots especially in crocus time - a graphic reminder of the dramatic change that the passage of time can bring.

# The Water Mills - Part I

## Bishopton and High Cleugh

When the original Riponians first chose to settle in these parts, one major attraction would have been easy access to running water - in particular the Laver and the Skell - and one of the benefits offered by those rivers was their ability to generate power via water mills - power which then could be harnessed for a variety of purposes. Building a working mill however required both capital outlay and control of the land through which the mill-race would run, and it is no surprise therefore to learn that in Ripon, the development of mills was the work of the Archbishop of York.

The main source of water for the Ripon mills was at Bishopton, where the Laver was tapped at High Dam up-river from Bishopton Bridge, and traces of the water channel can still be found, skilfully converted into an aqueduct (over a river loop) and then a culvert (under the main road) on its journey to Bishopton Mill.

The Archbishop's mill at Bishopton is recorded as early as 1305. By 1531 it was a fulling mill called 'Bishopton Walkemyll', interestingly at a time when Ripon's cloth industry was already in decline. It was later converted into a corn mill, but a flax mill was added close by in 1792, and its hemp was later worked in a rope walk next door. The Waite family were corn millers there for some years in the mid-19thC, and William Atkinson was the flax spinner. By 1909 a saw mill is recorded too, but drastic change was at hand. A disastrous fire in June 1915 which troops from the nearby Army Camp could only watch, destroyed the flax mill and took

away 60 jobs, mostly of women and girls, and by the 1920s the corn mill too was disused - primarily however as a result of the advent of new technology.

Another of the Archbishop's engineering feats lay a little east of Bishopton Mills, where the Laver was dammed at High Cleugh in the early Middle Ages to serve a mill-race of extraordinary length which ran down into Ripon and is the subject of a later article. Despite the Laver flow, High Cleugh dam needed topping up from the Skell, and not far from where the Fairy Steps now stand, Skell Crooks dam was constructed to divert water along a special channel into High Cleugh dam.

Skell Crooks may well date back to early medieval times, but complications arose centuries later when Ripon Canal (Navigation) was opened, drawing its water from the Skell at the foot of Bedern Bank. Too much water diverted into High Cleugh dam would have left the Skell depleted, especially in dry weather, so a limit was set on the height of Skell Crooks dam to ensure this did not happen. A metal plate dated 1820, fixed on a stone block nearby, set the level of the dam as being 7 feet below the marker. Unfortunately the plaque was stolen some years ago but photographs of it survive.

For centuries the dams were faithfully repaired after repeated flood damage since men's livelihood depended on them, but by the end of the 19thC more efficient forms of power and better food transportation combined to make water-powered mills less profitable, and as the Ripon mill dams suffered their periodic natural disasters it became uneconomic to repair them and they gradually fell into disuse.

## The Water Mills - Part II

### High Mill and Duck Hill Mill

The Archbishop of York's medieval water mills in Ripon began with the Laver dammed at High Cleugh to serve a lengthy millrace that flowed down towards the town along the line now followed by Mallorie Park Drive and Skellbank.

The first task of the water was to turn the wheel at High Mill, now the site of Hugh Ripley Hall, where millstones can still be seen outside set in the ground. In its day the mill consisted of a large complex of buildings that jutted well out into Skellbank, and included stables, cart sheds and two mill-workers cottages. It was described in its last years by an eye-witness as a stone building of four floors with a grey slate roof and the usual hoist tackle for raising heavy sacks; the mill-wheel, like all the others, was undershot. Children played their risky games in the mill-race, particularly in hot weather, and watched the carts arrive and depart.

High Mill, sometimes called Skellbank Mill and probably the West Mill recorded in 1531, seems always to have been a corn mill, but in 1776 premises for a paper mill are said to have been added to it by Christopher Pinckney, the then miller. However, when the dam at High Cleugh was destroyed by floods in 1892, High Mill would have ground to an abrupt and permanent halt. The buildings were demolished in 1902.

From High Mill the mill-race flowed on down Somerset Row and Water

old Duck Hill Mill, Ripon.

Skellgate as an open channel except where crossed by bridges. At the end of Water Skellgate it broadened into a pond outside Duck Hill Mill, known in the Middle Ages as Byemilne, another possession of the Archbishop and first recorded in 1228. At that time it was almost certainly the Norman borough's main corn mill and users had to pay the Archbishop's tolls. Although corn-grinding remained its prime function, for nearly a hundred years after 1776, through the efforts of William Askwith, it also housed an engine that pumped water from the mill-race up into town where it was distributed by pipes for domestic use.

For many years in the early/mid 19thC the mill was run by the Gatenby family. Its active life ended in 1892, if not a little earlier, with the collapse of High Cleugh dam, but the advent of steam-powered roller milling had already sealed the fate of water-powered corn mills.

The open water course which gave Water Skellgate its name was bridged over in 1875 at a cost of £400, and its existence was no doubt largely forgotten after the mill closed until one day the tunnel roof collapsed under the weight of the 'Wakeman' steam roller, to the entertainment of boys from nearby Jepson's School. Incidents like this probably gave rise to the legend of a tunnel to Fountains Abbey.

The water course along Skellgarths was vaulted over somewhat earlier, but was similarly liable to damage from heavy vehicles. In 1883 the Corporation borrowed £800 in order to rebuild the whole mill-race roof from Duck Hill Mill to Union Mill, at the foot of Bedern Bank.

## The Water Mills - Part III

### Union Mill and Low Mill

As the Archbishop's lengthy mill-race flowed eastwards from its origin at High Cleugh, serving two mills en route, it eventually reached yet another mill at the foot of Bedern Bank near the present roundabout.

In its final years it was known as Union Mill, the name taken from the private company that ran it in the late 19thC, with an office and warehouse in King St.

A little earlier, William Peacock had been miller there for more than 20 years. In the 14thC however the Archbishop had had a fulling mill on this site where heavy hammers (previously feet!) had compacted woollen cloth, but after the decline of the local cloth industry in early Tudor times the 'Walkemylle' appears

to have been turned over to grinding corn, as at Bishopton. Even so the mill could not survive the failure of High Cleugh dam in 1892 and has now disappeared without trace, though a little lower down, by Bondgate Green Bridge, a modern drain outlet in the banks of the Skell marks the point where in the 19thC the mill's tail-race returned its water to the river.

This however had not always been the case. When first constructed in the early Middle Ages the mill race at the foot of Bedern Bank had headed for the strip of land - now private gardens - between High St. Agnesgate and the Skell, and then further on had flowed along Low Mill road, where the open water course could still be seen not many years ago. The dating evidence is confusing, but at some point in the 18thC, the decision was taken to block off the High St Agnesgate section, and run the mill-race into the Skell close to Union Mill (see above). However, at the end of Low Mill road there were still two mills requiring water and by 1800 a new dam (later known as Alma Weir) had been constructed across the Skell to divert water into the earlier mill race down Low Mill road.

This left the High St. Agnesgate water course presumably out of use. Eventually it was forgotten, only to be accidentally re-discovered from time to time in years to come, as in the garden of St. Agnes Lodge in 2000 where it survives as a brick-vaulted tunnel, some three feet wide and nearly four feet high to

the apex, with side walls of cobble and ashlar blocks. In 2003 the watercourse was located in the garden of Thorpe Prebend House, but this section proved to have a stone vaulted roof. As late as 1772 this stretch of mill-race is marked on maps as an open water-course - a stream through the gardens - with crossing points. So why was it neatly vaulted over in its final days? No answer is yet available.

Low Mill was sited at the end of Priest Lane, near the ford. This is close to Ripon's original Saxon heartland, and is likely to be the mill referred to in Domesday Book (1086) as belonging – inevitably - to the Archbishop. If so, the mill would have had its own local dam, later destroyed. By 1221 it was called the East Mill, and was plugged into the Archbishop's new mill-race bringing water down from High Cleugh to the town. Throughout its long life it remained a corn mill, surviving in use with the help of Alma Weir until as late as 1938. From the 1830s there was a second Low Mill, nearer Fishergreen, at first used for bone-grinding, later as a saw mill.

For close on a thousand years water mills were an essential part of the Ripon scene - their passing must be noted with sadness.

# Bondgate Brewery

## That distinctive aroma

This picture of brewery workers about to take part in the Millenary Festival of 1886 is a reminder that there were once breweries in Ripon. This one was located in Bondgate, on the banks of the Skell, where Waterside residents now live, and it is likely that the Skell both provided fresh water and took away the waste. The name in the early 19thC of the Crown Steam Brewery indicates that it had already adopted the new technology of the age, and its very tall chimney no doubt served as one of the landmarks of the town.

The founder of the business appears to have been Richard Lumley, described in 1823 as a 'common brewer' in Bondgate. He developed the brewery

and ran it until his death at 85 in 1862, no doubt increasingly helped by his son also called Richard, who then took over.

By the time his father died Richard Lumley junior was already a City Councillor, and he went on to become three times Mayor of Ripon (1874-5, 1875-6 and 1880-1). In 1883 he died at the age of

55, by which time the business had become a limited company, Richard Lumley & Co., advertised as 'maltsters and ale and porter brewers'.

Despite Lumley's death, given his record of public service, it was inevitable that the Crown Brewery would wish to be actively involved in the great Millenary Festival (1886), and in addition to providing a float for the procession, we are told that the company set up a large imitation crown, illuminated at night, to decorate the entrance to the brewery yard.

Thomas Hepworth from Skipton now headed the business which was soon renamed Hepworth & Co., and after his death in 1892 Richard Wilkinson was managing director for a decade. In 1896 the brewery was much enlarged, and maltkilns (for drying the barley) were acquired in North Road. By Edwardian times Hepworth's Brewery had an office in Queen Street and no doubt supplied most of Ripon's public houses. It can be assumed that vast quantities of its beer were consumed by the thousands of soldiers who were based in Ripon during World War One - in July 1919 Hepworth's contributed 100 gallons of beer for a celebratory dinner in the Market Place for the soldiers still here!

That same year Hepworth's acquired the *Unicorn* Hotel, but times were changing and, with the growth of the major brewery companies after the Second World War, Hepworth's was taken over by Vaux. In 1957 it was decided to cease beer production in Bondgate, and use the plant for storage only. Soon however the brewery connection ceased altogether and in 1970 the site was taken by Econ Engineering.

Only one building has survived the dramatic structural changes since then; at the entrance to the Waterside complex still stands what used to be Hepworth's office, next to the *Bricksetters' Arms*, where deliveries of Hepworth's Ales were no doubt always guaranteed!


# The Tannery

### Not nice for the neighbours
There were many uses for leather in the 19thC, from saddles and harnesses to drive belts for machinery. Such was the demand, every town would have its tannery and Victorian Ripon had at least two - one located in Black Swan Yard off Westgate, and the other off High St. Agnesgate on the banks of the Skell, seen in the picture here with chimney, engine house, sheds and workshops. In tanneries animal hides were converted into leather by going through various processes which included scraping the skins and soaking them in solutions of tannin derived from oak bark (which gave tanneries their characteristic foul smell).

Trade directories reveal that the tannery by the Skell was in operation by 1826 when it was run by one Nicholas Yorke. By 1842 ownership of the business had passed to William Yorke (his son?), a magistrate and Mayor of Ripon in 1854-5. Until his death in 1877 he lived near the works in what is now Alma House. By then however the tannery had been acquired by James Ostcliffe, and a map of 1891 shows the cluster of cottages known as Ostcliffe's Court lying immediately to the east. However, by the time James Ostcliffe died in 1885 (aged 40) the tannery had closed down, hit no doubt like many others by technological change within the industry.

At this stage the Trees family, long established in Ripon as builders, enter the story. An Isaac Trees, bricklayer, is recorded as early as 1814, when his daughter was baptised. He also had a son James (d.1888) who eventually took over the family business which was first located in Stonebridgegate, then in Hall Yard off Kirkgate in the 1870s, and later in St. Marygate.

In 1885 the Trees family acquired the site of the tannery, and in 1902 the business moved to High St. Agnesgate, now led by James' nephew, Abel Trees. Work soon began on the construction of Skellfield Terrace and Abel took up residence there himself. After his death in 1930 the business was run by his son, his grandson, and now by his great-grandson, but the title of A.B. Trees & Son has been retained.

For many years the outlook from Skellfield Terrace was dominated by the Alma Weir which channelled water from the river down a stone-lined millrace to Low Mill at the end of Priest Lane, a mill which had originated in the early Middle Ages. Alma Weir however is no earlier than the 18thC. Before then, Low Mill drew its water supply from the same town mill-race which served mills at Duck Hill and at the foot of Bedern Bank before flowing east through the gardens of Thorpe Prebend and the other houses along High St. Agnesgate. The discovery in 2000 and 2003 of stretches of this fine vaulted channel, strangely abandoned many years ago, serves as a reminder that further along, on its way to Low Mill Road, it would have run under Yorke's Tannery buildings and still no doubt runs under part of Skellfield Terrace.

The picturesque sprawl of tannery buildings attracted the attention of artists in Victorian times as the engraving reminds us. What we are less aware of are the aromas that would have been encountered on a walk along the Skell in those days, generated by the paint and varnish works, the brewery and then the tannery! And if the tannery had gone by the 1890s, the sewage works at Fisher Green was about to arrive.

# Ripon Loyal Volunteers

## Meritorious zeal and indefatigable exertions

In the past, when the country has been thought to be under threat, defence groups have sprung up to protect their locality, most famously the Home Guard in 1940, and Ripon has played its full part in these activities. In the 1790s the feared enemy was Revolutionary France, soon to achieve the domination of Europe under the Emperor Napoleon, and for nearly twenty years Britain felt itself in danger of either internal revolution or external invasion.

In Ripon there was a surprisingly fast reaction to this perceived threat. In June 1794 a public meeting was held to consider what needed to be done, and it was decided that funds should be raised to form a corps of infantry at least 60 strong. Local worthies contributed money generously, the newly formed unit was named the Ripon Loyal Volunteer Company, and a search was made for a sergeant, a drummer and a fifer.

The commanding officer was Captain John Dalton, aged 36, of Sleningford Park, from a long-established family with a strong military tradition. Presumably some intensive basic training of the new volunteer recruits was undertaken, and in 1798 the Company bravely declared itself ready to march to any part of England where their services could be used. This offer however was not taken up, and the unit turned instead to more leisurely pursuits; in July 1800, after coming successfully through an inspection by a visiting Colonel on Ripon Common, the officers took their guest off to the *Unicorn* for 'an elegant entertainment'.

Captain Dalton was clearly held in high regard by his men, since by 1800 they had presented him with a silver cup worth 50 guineas. Interestingly, a silver cup of slightly later date (1807) still survives, inscribed in honour of a John Horne, Captain and Adjutant of the Ripon Loyal Volunteers, and praising him for 'Meritorious Zeal and Indefatigable Exertions' in promoting the discipline of the Regiment. Obviously a martinet with the common touch.

By then the worst crisis of the Napoleonic War had come and gone; in 1804, with invasion threatening, Dalton, now a Lieutenant Colonel, had offered the services of his riflemen (nearly 100) to the Government, but were told that the quota of West Riding Volunteers was complete. However more local recognition was at hand. In June 1805 Ripon Corporation assembled in their gowns at Borrage Bridge

to meet the Volunteers returning from duty in Leeds; after parade on the Square, the Corporation and Officers then dined at the Town Hall. A few months later, the new commanding officer Lieut. Col. Wood and his officers celebrated another successful inspection with a dinner at the *Unicorn*, the evening concluding with 'the utmost conviviality and mirth'.

Loyal Volunteers were one thing, but the Regulars were another. In January 1810 Ripon innkeepers complained bitterly about soldiers being quartered upon them - the 68th Regiment in 1806-7, and then the 15th Regiment later. It is likely that relief came only with Waterloo and the end of the war. Lieut. Colonel Dalton however lived to be 83, reminiscing no doubt in later years over the exciting 'Home Guard' experiences of his youth.


# Belgian Refugees

## Political asylum in an earlier age

The Kosovan refugees accommodated in Ripon in the late 1990s were not the first victims of war to find a safe haven in the ancient city. Late in 1914 the tide of battle in the First World War flowed through Belgium, and thousands fled their country to escape it.

Belgium had not even been involved in the Great Power alliances which preceded the war, but its geographical position drew it into the conflict. The German war plan required the early defeat of France before ponderous Russia had fully mobilised its strength, and the best chance of achieving that was to invade France via the easy terrain of Belgium. Britain, as a guarantor of Belgian independence, felt it had no alternative but to declare war on Germany.

Even the combined strength of the British, French and Belgian forces, however, could not halt the German onslaught in August 1914, and the retreat from Mons left almost the whole of Belgium in German hands. Many civilians fled their country in advance of the invaders, and over one hundred thousand crossed the Channel to England.

There the mood was one of great sympathy for 'brave little Belgium', and the refugees were duly distributed to towns and villages around the

country. Harrogate eventually took over 350 and Ripon received over 40. Rent-free accommodation had to be found for them and duly was, in Park Street, Heath's Court, Bondgate, Coltsgate Hill, Stonebridgegate and even at the Spa Hotel. Food, fuel and clothing were liberally donated, and much money raised for the

Belgian Relief Fund via concerts and special events.

No one person in Ripon did more to help them than Father Ernest Levick, priest-in-charge at St. Wilfrid's church, who knew their country, spoke Flemish, and felt responsible for all the Roman Catholics among them. He raised money on their behalf, gave talks on Belgium, and helped teach their children in St Wilfrid's school. After the war he received a special award from the Belgian ambassador in recognition of his services.

The refugees naturally wanted to put their time to good use and support themselves, and found a way of doing this through toy-making. In a workshop in Park Street they used old wooden cigar boxes to make a variety of toys, their speciality being Noah's Arks. These were displayed in a Market Place shop window, orders were taken, and by the end of November 1914 fifteen had been ordered at a guinea each. The idea aroused much interest in Harrogate, and early in 1915 a Noah's ark was sent to Queen Mary at her request (see picture).

Interestingly, an example of this popular line came to light in 1998 when an elderly lady, born in Ripon but living in Suffolk, presented to Mayor Barry Kay the Ark which had been in her family since 1914. It bears the crossed flags of Britain and Belgium, but also the Ripon Horn.

# The First World War Army Camp

## Ripon becomes a garrison town

A photograph of a column of soldiers marching down High Skellgate is an instant reminder of the great impact of the First World War on Ripon and its surroundings. Although in the years before the war Territorial Army units had set up their tents on Red Bank, where the Victorian racecourse had once been, there had been nothing previously on the scale of the great camp that was created in 1915.

This 1000-acre site dominated Ripon's outskirts to the west and south, stretching in a huge swathe from Kirkby Road to the Harrogate Road, taking in long stretches of the Laver and Skell and even reaching as far out as Studley Roger.

Miles of new roads and footpaths had to be laid, and to service the camp a special light railway was constructed, branching from the main line at Littlethorpe and crossing the Harrogate Road near where Safeways now stands.

Special arrangements had to be made to provide

the water required (over half a million gallons a day) and two great reservoir tanks were set up. New drains had to be laid to get the sewage down to the treatment works at Fishergreen, a special power station was built to provide the Camp with electricity, and rows and rows of barrack huts appeared.

The camp was constructed by an army of workmen, many of whom came into the town in the evenings to drink, startling local residents and keeping the magistrates busy. In May 1915 the labourers gave way to soldiers as the first Durham Light Infantry and West Yorkshire battalions arrived, and soon there were to be soldiers in Ripon in their thousands. They too came into the town for recreation and found it; in addition to the pubs there was a rest and refreshment room in the Temperance Hall on Duck Hill, whilst the YMCA, the Mission Hall in Water Skellgate and the churches in general worked hard to meet the men's needs.

The town had already contributed to the war effort itself. Recruitment meetings had been held in the Square with speeches from the Town Hall balcony, and the dilapidated Wakeman's House found use as a recruiting centre. Then there were Belgian refugees to accommodate, and the first wounded returned from the front, but it was the arrival of droves of soldiers in the town which no doubt had the greatest impact. It was boom time not only for the pubs (after 6 pm) but also for the cinemas which opened in Kirkgate and Water Skellgate. Scottish soldiers however could provide entertainment of their own, as in April 1916; archive film survives of their Military Sports and Highland Games on the racecourse in front of appreciative spectators. A captured German gun was set up in the Square for people to stare at, and in August a bugler from the Cameron Highlanders caused surprise by blowing the Horn at the obelisk. Early in 1918 the war-poet Wilfred Owen found inspiration for his work while stationed in Ripon for several weeks.

Shops too did well out of their new customers. Several came to advertise the army services that they provided - officers' equipment, the cleaning of uniforms, coffee for the officers' mess and even fruit and flowers. The Lawrence Restaurant offered 'Special Accommodation for Officers'! The ending of the war in November 1918, like the outbreak, was the cause of great excitement and there was much rejoicing and celebration - despite the flu epidemic. The war was over, but Ripon and the Armed Forces had formed a lasting bond.


# Spurriers and Spurs

### Fame for the city

Ripon's best known product over the years, apart from paint and varnish, has been the rowel spur, which enjoyed a national reputation in the 17th and 18thC. "As true steel as Ripon rowels" was a catchphrase of those times, and the industry is still commemorated today in such names as the Rowel Players, the Ripon Rowels Handicap and the Rotary Club of Ripon Rowels.

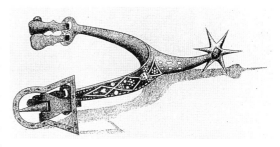

Rowel spurs with their eye-catching spiked wheels came into use in the 14thC, and in the Age of Chivalry were part of the trappings of knighthood, awarded when that honour was bestowed and occasionally stripped from knights in disgrace. But by Tudor times spurs were more generally available, valued for their practical use as well as being regarded as a fashionable status symbol. It was then that their manufacture would have begun in Ripon.

Certainly by 1607 spurriers are mentioned in Ripon in local records, and were then part of a metal-workers guild which enforced the usual guild rules - only members could practise their trade in the town but first they were required to pay subscription fees to take up their 'freedom'. Guilds appointed 'searchers' whose job was to ensure that no 'foreigners' brought illegal competition to the town without being fined.

In the late 17thC a plain pair of steel spurs cost a shilling, but a decorated pair was as much as 7 shillings and 6 pence. As special gifts they could even be inlaid with silver, and it was doubtless such sets that were given to the Archbishop of York in 1685 and 1694. Earlier that century, in April 1617, a lavish pair of 'Rippon spurres' had been presented to King James I himself when he visited Ripon, and they were "such a contentmente to his Majestie as his Highness did weare the same the following day at his departure".

The names of Ripon spurriers are recorded sporadically from Jacobean times onwards, but most is known about the last of them, John Terry, who died in 1798. Terry was admitted a freeman in 1738 and soon afterwards joined Ripon Corporation. By 1761 he had become an Alderman, and was then elected Mayor, first in 1762-3 and again in 1773-4. Obviously a popular choice, he completed his hat-trick by becoming Mayor a third time in 1786-7. Terry's home and workshop lay on the south side of the Square, where the Yorkshire Bank now stands. When he died in 1798 in his ninetieth year, the craft apparently died with him, having fallen victim to changing fashions.

A century earlier John Aislabie had rightly placed a giant rowel spur on the top of the Obelisk (1702) to celebrate the fact that spur manufacture had brought fame to Ripon. For 200 years the Spur was to rival the Horn as the symbol of the town.

As local industries rise and fall in our own day, it is important to remember that Ripon was once pre-eminent in this specialist field. Fortunately an original example of this skill in craftsmanship still survives in the Town Hall among the City treasures.

# Postcards and Letters

## Messages from the past

The sending of letters and postcards to and from Ripon has been going on for well over a century, and until quite recent times they bore the local frankmark - even villages such as Galphay, Kirklington, Kirkby Malzeard and Snape had their own, along with Ripon, Bedale and Northallerton.

A hundred years ago the sending of postcards was a national pastime. They were produced to highlight the attractions of their chosen area in order to entice more visitors. The two postcards shown here, as well as appealing for visitors, have a central drop-down section which provides a dozen or more small pictures of local beauty spots.

The modern collector however is attracted to these postcards not just by the views but by their hand-written messages. This can vary from the banal to the intriguing, but none has yet been found which actually says 'Wish You Were Here!'

Many messages leave us with the frustration of wanting to know What Happened Next? They abound in snippets of personal information. One sent from Galphay in October 1913 by a young girl to a lady in Harrogate thanks her for a box of chocolates and hair ribbon for her birthday, and mentions that the postman was called Jim Richmond. Another, written at Kirklington Hall to a friend or relative in Masham, was probably from a maid who had just started work as she states that "I did not intend leaving home just yet".

Other messages not surprisingly complain about the weather - "the weather is still wet - it is sickening'" (1917) - but a card of 1905 to Halifax describes Ripon as "a pretty place" and states that the writer was enjoying "glorious weather". Postcards were sent not only by casual visitors but by students at the College and soldiers at the great Army Camp during the First World War. One such, 'George', wrote in 1915 to his mother in Hull, complaining about the state of the cheesecakes he had received from home and requesting

instead for "your poor little lad who is hungry" a few currant cakes which "go hard and good". Almost all the rest of the message was about food.

On a much later postcard (1951) depicting the Hornblower, an uncle and aunt wrote to their niece in Harrogate, describing the ceremony which they had just witnessed for the first time:

"There's a free concert in the Market Place every evening at 9.00. This man is the guest artist - but he doesn't blow his own trumpet".

In addition to postcards, many private letters survive from even earlier times, and can sometimes be bought at collectors' fairs. Far from containing good wishes, these are often about unpaid bills, mainly perhaps because they are nearly always to or from solicitors. Occasionally however something special surfaces - such as the donation of a collection of some 900 Victorian letters, exchanged between Robert Williamson - of Ripon's famous paint and varnish works - and the lady from near Malton who became his wife. An exciting discovery by any standard, full of family interest, and now after careful study safely lodged at North Yorkshire County Record Office.

# North Bridge

## Battered but unbroken

Arguably North Bridge comes second only to the Cathedral as Ripon's finest medieval structure. Before its construction, travellers coming to Ripon from the North had to cross the ford a little downstream from the later bridge or make a major detour if the river was high. But when the Archbishop of York had the Market Place laid out as part of his new Borough in the 12thC, the needs of commerce required an all-weather link with the outside world to the north, and a stone bridge across the Ure became a necessity.

The flood plain of the river at this point is very wide, as we know in our own day, and the new bridge had to be of great length to span it, incorporating a multiplicity of arches. At least one of these, near the Sharow bank on the downstream side, still displays a profusion of medieval masons' marks on its underside. Hard evidence of the bridge's existence comes in 1228 with the earliest reference yet found to the street named Stonebridgegate.

By the 15thC a chapel to the little-known St Sitha stood on the bridge and offerings were left there toward its upkeep (11s.1d. in 1478). Bridge maintenance was always a problem given the regular Ure floods - bequests were made in wills towards the bridge's upkeep and tolls were levied on users (in 1358 1d. per cartload of

corn, 1d. per 20 sheep and a farthing per cow) but in post-medieval times responsibility for the bridge came to rest firmly with the magistrates meeting in Quarter Sessions.

In the early 17thC the river divided the North from the West Riding, which provided ample opportunity for the County Magistrates to bicker over maintenance costs. In James I's reign the bridge was badly in need of repair, and after a long wrangle it was finally decided that it was entirely the responsibility of the West Riding. But the problem was ongoing. Thomas Gent's *History of Ripon* records that in February 1733 "great floods, one, the highest that was known in the memory of man, did great damage to North Bridge - the water being close to the arches ran over with fierce impetuosity at both ends, drowning abundance of cattle and sheep, carrying away haystacks, etc."

Then as today there were regular accidents involving vehicles. In 1774 the *York Courant* reported that when Richard Pickersgill's stage waggon from Newcastle was passing over the North Bridge the axletree broke, throwing the waggon over the parapet into a field. One horse was killed and the other badly injured. In 1821 flood water washed a great hole in one of the arches, and in the dark the *Telegraph* stagecoach, also from Newcastle, narrowly escaped disaster when it missed the hole by inches.

The siting of the railway station north of the river (1848) further increased the importance of the bridge, and soon an omnibus service was shuttling people to and from town. However, Old North Bridge was deemed inadequate to take this extra traffic, and in 1880-1 it was doubled in width as part of a general North Road improvement scheme spearheaded by Mayor Collinson. Much of the cost was raised by public subscription. Some years later, during the First World War, the bridge successfully withstood the tramp of marching men as soldiers in their thousand headed from the trains to the town and army camp. But by the close of the 20thC the closure of the railway and the opening of the Bypass meant that North Bridge could enjoy quieter times.

# Hewick Bridge

## When bridge chapels were commonplace

Hewick Bridge, like North Bridge, crosses the Ure, but in this case provides Ripon with a vital communication link to the east rather than to the north, and this route from Ripon to York must have been in use as early as the days of the much travelled St Wilfrid.

The original bridge would have been of timber and not of exceptional length, since there is no wide flood plain to cross at this point, but it would have been regularly exposed to the full force of the Ure in spate, and doubtless suffered accordingly. For this reason a more substantial bridge of stone was to be preferred but this could only be provided by an authority with wealth and power. Such was

the Archbishop of York, and his interest in Ripon would have increased significantly with the founding of his borough in the 12thC.

As previously noted, the newly established Market Place was an active commercial centre that required good transport links with the outside world (soon particularly for its cloth industry) and it is likely that the first stone Hewick Bridge, like North Bridge, had been constructed by 1200 or even a little before. The first reference to it found so far is in 1358, by which time it was already in need of repair.

Royal approval was given that year for bridge tolls to be levied for a specified period to raise the necessary funds (a penny for a cartload of corn, a halfpenny for 10 sheep, etc), and again like North Bridge, Hewick Bridge also enjoyed an income from regular bequests. William Wrampan left 5 shillings for its maintenance in 1466; other bequests are recorded in 1371, 1376, 1488, 1505, 1515 and 1535. Similarly there was an income of sorts from voluntary offerings left at the bridge chapel (dedicated to St. Anthony) - ten and a half pence when the box was opened in 1478. In 1532 the chapel itself required repairs, and is described as being "at the end of the bridge" (almost certainly the north end). There is also reference to a hermit living there - perhaps he guarded the offertory box?

A few years later, Henry Vlll's roving antiquary John Leland visited Ripon and mentioned "Hewik bridge of stone on Ure" with its "fair chapel of freestone". In 1697 another traveller, this time a lady, Celia Fiennes, made some interesting observations: "There are two good bridges to the town, one was a rebuilding, pretty large, with several arches, called Hewet bridge. It is often out of repair by reason of the force of the water that swells after great raines; yet I see they made works of wood on purpose to break the violence of the stream; and the middle arch is very large and high".

By the 18thC responsibility for maintaining (and periodically rebuilding) the bridge had passed from the Church to the magistrates of the West Riding, and their County Council successors in later times were to find that with large motorised vehicles, despite some widening, the relative narrowness of the bridge and the sharp turns at either end can still lead to damage to the parapet work. In addition, during times of heavy rain, the bridge can be closed by flooding near the racecourse, whilst in the summer crowds of drinkers crossing the bridge from the *Black-a-Moor* pub are also a hazard to be negotiated!

# Laver and Skell road bridges

## Spanning the decades

Bridges have always been of great importance to Ripon, virtually surrounded as it is by Laver, Skell and Ure. In addition to North Bridge and Hewick Bridge across the Ure, Ripon's communication links also require bridges across the Laver and Skell for those journeying to the west and south.

The historic road to the west, to Fountains Abbey, Pateley Bridge and Studley Royal, crossed the Laver at Bishopton where a stone bridge is recorded as early as the 14thC, complete with chapel (to St. Mary) and offertory box - in 1478 the box produced 10 pence towards maintenance costs. Offerings were augmented by the usual bequests (e.g. in 1459 William Foster left 2 shillings for the bridge). Bridge chapels attracted hermits who sometimes turned out to be rascals - in 1525 the Bishopton Bridge hermit had to be removed and was imprisoned in York. In later times responsibility for maintenance passed from the Church to the West Riding Justices, and they arranged for the bridge to be doubled in width in 1885.

After the Laver joins the Skell, the first stone bridge to be encountered downstream is now called Borrage Bridge, but in medieval times it was known as Esegel (Skell) Bridge and is mentioned in 1343. There was no hermit in this case, but the customary maintenance bequests are recorded (e.g. 3 shillings 4 pence left by William Wrampan in 1466, 20 pence by John Pigott in 1488). It was built of stone by the 1530s, and may already have been so for many years. South of the bridge lay the open fields, common pastures and the trackway to Markenfield Hall (via Whitcliffe Lane) and beyond.

From the 17thC however, the bridge's name changed, evolving through various forms to Burgage, then Borrage Bridge, and it was the burgesses who helped repair it in the 17thC. However, standards were slipping, and in 1765 the Corporation had to pay for the ruinous bridge to be rebuilt, now a key element on the new turnpike road to Harrogate and Leeds.

Yet further downstream stood Bondgate Bridge, important since early times since it connected Bondgate to the town as well as carrying Ripon's main road south (to Knaresborough). In 1459 the bridge received 6 pence in a maintenance

bequest, another 2 shillings in 1466, and 3 shillings and 4 pence in 1488. Surprisingly, by the early 16thC the bridge was still of timber but in 1745 it was rebuilt as a graceful stone structure with three arches, and as such it survived for nearly 150 years. However in 1892, when it was in need of widening and repair, the Victorians' love of iron and steel triumphed, and with much pomp and ceremony a metal successor was constructed and opened.

Nowadays however it is in a weakened condition, as drivers are warned, and it does not compare favourably with the next bridge downstream, nearly a hundred years older but still fit and well. This is Bondgate Green Bridge, hump-backed and in stone, built in 1809-10 next to the ancient ford where the road to York crossed the river. By Regency times busy stagecoaches could not be delayed by a turbulent Skell, but perhaps the initiative for change came from Dean Waddilove who is reputed to have been nearly drowned in his coach one night when crossing the ford on returning from Newby. No doubt the new bridge also greatly eased the movement of freight to and from the canal basin. Ripon is fortunate to be so well endowed with historic river bridges.

## Skell Footbridges

### Meeting local needs

In addition to the various road bridges across the Skell in Ripon, there have long been a number of footbridges too, serving the needs of travellers and local residents.

The Rustic Bridge at High Cleugh, built of intertwined branches, was colourfully illustrated on Edwardian postcards in its idyllic leafy setting at the confluence of the Laver and Skell. It doubtless suffered during the First World War from the boots of many soldiers trekking to and from the Army Camp at Red Bank, but it was worse damaged by the great flood of August 1927. In later years it reappeared in an all-metal format that survived until the early 1980s, then being replaced by the present graceful timber structure (still on a metal base) which continues to offer a useful short-cut on the western edge of the town.

Much further downstream there had long been a need for townsfolk to enjoy an easy crossing of the Skell into Bondgate Green without having to thread their way through Bondgate itself. Among those heading for the Green were the local bowmen, wishing to practise their skills, and by the 15thC (if not earlier) Archer bridge, lying between Thorpe Prebend House and St. Anne's Hospital, had been built to serve their needs. The Hospital (or Maison Dieu) offered a wayfarer's dole plus a bed for the night to poor travellers on foot or horseback from further afield. No doubt the bread came from legacies such as the one in 1484 of an annual

bushel of corn, left to the Hospital by Robert Horsman of Littlethorpe, doubtless a regular bridge user. Archer Bridge also attracted the usual maintenance bequests, e.g. 3 shillings and 4 pence by John Pigott in 1488.

This timber footbridge was renewed, certainly not for the first time, by John Aislabie in 1717, but then in 1754 it was rebuilt in stone at the expense of the Corporation. Unfortunately no illustration of this stone bridge appears to survive, and some 50 years later it was dismantled and removed when Bondgate Green road bridge was built a short distance upstream (1809-10). The stone flagged bases of the piers of Archer Bridge can still be seen in the river bed in the summer and part of an arch survives in the cellar of the bandroom.

Further downstream is busy Alma footbridge, whose superstructure was transformed from concrete into elegant timberwork in 2001. Built in concrete in the early 1960s, it replaced a timber bridge constructed some hundred years before, c.1862, by Thomas Stubbs, former Master of the House of Correction, who retired to this part of the town and named his new bridge after the Crimean War battle that so captivated him. The view of the Cathedral with Alma footbridge in the foreground became one of the classic views of Ripon in Edwardian times, as surviving postcards show. In 2001 a Lottery grant made possible the bridge's return to timber, along with various other improvements along this stretch of the Skell.

Finally, next door to the only remaining ford (and probably the most ancient) across the Skell, is Woodbridge at the end of Firs Avenue. It is first marked on a map of 1818 and, periodically renewed, it has offered a convenient all-weather river crossing on the eastern outskirts of the town.

# St. Anne's Hospital

### A welcome break for wayfarers

St. Anne's may be the smallest of Ripon's three medieval hospitals but it is certainly not the least interesting. Although its origins are obscure, it was probably founded in the 12thC, giving its name to the street Annesgate (also known as St.Agnesgate), mentioned as early as 1228. It appears however to have been a private rather than a church foundation.

In medieval times its purpose was to house eight poor folk (men *and* women) who were also elderly, infirm, of Christian character and "honest behaviour". There was a resident priest to say Mass in the chapel and there were two common beds for impoverished overnight travellers. The travellers in question would be those coming from the south, entering the town via Archer footbridge over the Skell, next to Thorpe Prebend House. No doubt the prospect of a free bed for the night and a hot drink by the great open fireplace helped to keep wayfarers going over the last long mile.

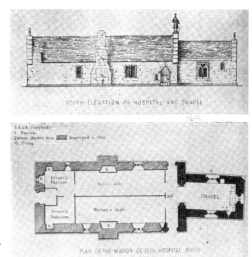

Like the other hospitals, St. Anne's (often referred to as the Maison Dieu) derived its income from donations, bequests, and the sale of indulgences (for forgiveness of sins). Land endowments were rare, but in 1623 a rent of 4 shillings a year was promised from a public house - the *Hat and Beaver* in Horsefair, better known today as the *White Horse* in North Street. Sir Solomon Swale may have been a benefactor in the 1660s (though much eroded, a coat of arms attributed to him is still visible in the outer wall); later bequests to the Hospital certainly came from John Terry (1798), the last of Ripon's spurriers, and from Henry Greenwood of West Lodge (1864).

By the late 17thC only women were allowed entry to the hospital, but in earlier times the 'nave' of the building was probably partitioned into two small dormitories (see plan) for men and women, whilst the priest had a parlour and bedroom at the west end of the building. There could have been little space for the wayfarers! However, by the early 19thC the removal of Archer Bridge no doubt meant fewer visitors.

Vacancies among the Almswomen were filled by the Mayor and Corporation until 1836 after which the Trustees of Ripon's Municipal Charities took over, and it fell to them to resolve the problems of the late 1860s. As at the other two hospitals there was suddenly money to spend - in 1869 generous gifts from the Greenwood sisters of West Lodge made it possible for the block of almshouse cottages to be built which we still see today, with their gardens running down to the river, but this improvement unfortunately involved the demolition of the living quarters of the medieval hospital. Only the chancel was left standing, and that without its roof, but it does still retain its medieval altar slab.

However, when the Hospital was inspected in 1897, the Almswomen were receiving 5 shillings a week, and all was deemed to be in good order. No doubt the ladies were enjoying their more spacious accommodation, and all the indications are that St. Anne's has continued to serve its almswomen well ever since. Clearly the character and appearance of all three of Ripon's medieval Hospitals has undergone major change over the centuries but they still remain havens of comfort and security in an uncertain world.

# St. John's Hospital

## Fluctuating fortunes over the years

The Hospital of St. John the Baptist, in its picturesque setting on the banks of the Skell, was built like St. Mary Magdalen's by the side of a busy approach road, but in this case the Hospital was also at the point where for centuries a bridge spanned the river, bringing wayfarers into Ripon from the south.

The Hospital is a very early foundation, begun by Thomas, Archbishop of York, between 1109 and 1114. Its income came from endowments of land, added to over the years, and its mission was to provide hospitality for poor travellers (bread, soup and a bed). But it also had an educational role, helping to support four or five poor scholars who might eventually train for the priesthood, and in the early 19thC it was converted into a school itself, as we shall see.

Details are known of several of the medieval Masters of the Hospital, but its history in those years appears fairly uneventful. Prior to 1547, when the Reformation ended the practice, the chapel was much used as a chantry where masses were said for the souls of those who had provided funding for this service. In 1570, in the aftermath of the failure of the Rising of the North (an attempt to save the old Catholic religion), Thomas Blackburn, the then master, was fined "for hearing masse in rebellion tyme" and was lucky not to suffer a worse fate. A later Master, John Bramhall (1625-34) won credit for staying to comfort plague victims, presumably during the bad local outbreak of 1625.

In the 1680s the Dean took on the role of Master of the Hospital, but this unfortunately inaugurated a period of neglect and decline. Services in the chapel ceased in 1723, and years later (1812) the disused chapel was converted into a Boys' National School and run as such until 1853. A report by the Charity Commissioners (1820) noted that the almshouse accommodation amounted to one small single-storeyed house in Bondgate with apartments for two sisters known as almswomen. With the chapel out of use, the chaplain not surprisingly was an absentee pluralist, and the Commissioners were critical of the way the Hospital's income was being used.

Dramatic change was however just around the corner. In 1866 the Hospitals' Board of Trustees was set up, and two years later the decayed medieval chapel was replaced by the sturdy Victorian structure that we see today, large enough to seat

200. This was somewhat excessive for the number the church secured a loyal following among the people of Bondgate which it retained for many years.

The chaplain was to have an annual stipend of £40, the two almswomen a regular weekly income, and provision was made to enlarge their numbers. In 1878 the newly built block of almshouses provided for six. New life had been put back into St. John's Hospital, and at the end of the century an inspection by the Charity Commission declared that all was in order, which no doubt continues to be the case over a hundred years on, but financial problems relating to maintenance, restoration and improvement are never long absent.

# St. Mary Magdalen's Hospital

## A refuge for lepers and blind priests

Ripon's three sets of ancient almshouses, called Hospitals, all occupied important roadside locations in the Middle Ages, none more so than the Hospital of St. Mary Magdalen. It was founded in the early years of the 12thC, and was situated at the northern end of the road later known as Stonebridgegate, which at that time led to a ford across the Ure. The foundation of the Hospital is earlier than either the Market Place or North Bridge.

The founder was Thurstan, Archbishop of York, better known for his later connection with Fountains Abbey, and the medieval chapel still has a Norman doorway of that period. Well endowed with land, the Hospital's income went to support a community of 'sisters' plus a chaplain, and special care (food and a bed) was to be given to lepers and blind priests. At one time there was a special leper house, but this was demolished when leprosy declined in the later Middle Ages. Poor people, ordinary wayfarers and no doubt pilgrims could also receive hospitality there. Lucky ones might get fish or venison as well as bread.

Further endowments were made during medieval times and there was income from tithes and bequests as well as rents. A survey of 1535 revealed that the Master of the Hospital enjoyed a mansion house, garden and orchard, and in his care were two priests and five poor laymen 'oppressed with age and disease'. Perhaps the most notable Master of these times was Marmaduke Bradley (d. 1553), the deposed Abbot of Fountains, who also lost his Prebend of Thorpe but hung on (just) to his post at St Mary Magdalen's.

Well over a century later, in 1674, the almshouse cottages, then decayed, were rebuilt by the Master, Dr. Richard Hooke, to accommodate six sisters and a chaplain. Hooke's block of cottages were on the west side of the road, and faced towards the chapel (see picture). They have not survived however because in the 1870s they in turn were replaced by the brick cottages at an angle to

St. Mary Magdalen's Hospital,

the road, still to be seen today. The layout of this block was clearly influenced by the new Victorian chapel which had appeared in 1868/9, a bequest from the Revd George Mason of Copt Hewick Hall. Doubtless well-intentioned, it left the Hospital with the ongoing challenge of maintaining two chapels, a problem that has proved insuperable in our own time.

Still further expansion followed - in 1892, six more almshouses in the Jacobean style were added on the east side of the road, near the Leper Chapel. About the same time an old property (the Master's house ?) abutting on the west end of the chapel itself was removed.

Since 1686 Deans have been Masters of the Hospital, and since the late 1860s there has been a Board of Trustees to supervise its finances and direct its affairs.

The medieval chapel, restored in the late 1980s, still retains many features of interest today - the Norman door arch, the Perpendicular east window, a lowside window perhaps for lepers, a fine wooden screen and a medieval altar slab. Although the Hospital has given up its Victorian chapel, it is pleasing to report that its medieval chapel is now receiving tender loving care from a recently formed Friends organisation.

# Holy Trinity Church

## A story of continuing change

Few would deny that the spire of Holy Trinity church is one of the great landmarks of the city, as visible from the approach roads as the cathedral itself; there is however a major difference in age in that Holy Trinity is less than two centuries old.

Thomas Kilvington, a distinguished local physician, died in September 1823 in his 92nd year, and in his will left £13,000 to his relative, the Revd Edward Kilvington M.A., for Christian purposes. The latter used the money to build Holy Trinity church, and was to be priest-in-charge there for eight years. His bust still survives, near the altar.

The foundation stone was laid in July 1826 on what was undoubtedly a major occasion. A procession from the Town Hall to the site was led by the band of the Yorkshire Hussars, followed by the Mayor and Corporation in their robes and a cluster of clergy in their canonicals. We are told that there was also 'a large body of the most respectable inhabitants'. The laying of the stone was done by Lord Grantham of Newby Hall who wielded a silver trowel to spread the mortar and a mallet to tap the lowered stone into place.

The Revd Edward Kilvington then took the opportunity to read an address in which he not surprisingly praised the merits of the Church of England. The weather was kind, and among those in attendance was Elizabeth Sophia Lawrence of Studley Royal, but curiously not the Dean, nor would he lend the Minster choir for the occasion. After the ceremony lavish refreshments were provided in the Town Hall by Mr Sharpin, landlord of the *Unicorn*. In October 1827, on completion, the new church was consecrated by the Archbishop of York.

Large enough to seat 900, it was designed by Thomas Taylor in the Early English style with a very distinctive cruciform plan, and a tall broach spire at the west end rather than over the crossing. The church also has a fine groined arched roof and an extensive crypt, but it has not been to everyone's liking. The historian J.R.Walbran, who lived nearby and is buried in the churchyard, called it an 'absurd and incongruous compilation'.

In the 1860s, alterations began, and the church's story since is one of change - rearrangements, restoration work, the addition of new fittings and furnishings and the removal of others. Over the years galleries have come and gone, the organ and font moved to new positions, the pews modernised, a pulpit added and choir stalls added and then taken out. One of the most important changes was to switch the main entrance to the church from the corner nearest to the crossroads to its present position beneath the tower.

The story of updating the church to meet new requirements continued at the end of the 20thC with the launch of the Holy Trinity Space Project, an ambitious scheme by any standard which would cost over a million pounds, though the money was raised with apparent ease. Radical changes included opening up the crypt for greater community use especially by school groups, removing the pews in the nave so that replacement chairs could be set out or stacked as required, and providing better access and catering facilities. Hopefully our Victorian forefathers would have accepted that needs change with the passage of time, and for churches that means to respond or decline.

# St. Wilfrid's Church

## Novel design and rich decoration

A little over thirty years after the consecration of Holy Trinity Church in 1827, another place of Christian worship was opened in the same part of the town, this time dedicated to St. Wilfrid, and of particular significance since it was the first Catholic church to be built in Ripon since the Reformation. Its arrival announced the fact that full religious toleration had at last been achieved.

As elsewhere, toleration had been a long time coming. The papal church, after dominating the life of medieval Ripon, had been brusquely set aside in the middle years of the 16thC, and after the failure of the Rising of the North (an armed attempt to save it in 1569), Roman Catholics survived only in fear and secrecy for many decades, at best being fined for not attending Anglican services, and at worst suffering martyrdom. In the Ripon area a small Catholic community managed to hold mass regularly near Bishop Thornton.

Although the 18thC Enlightenment awoke a new interest in religious toleration, it was only in the early 19thC that legal discrimination against Roman Catholics was ended, allowing Catholic churches to be built again after a lapse of centuries. Tradition has it that in the 1850s a warehouse in Heath's Court off Low Skellgate was used for Catholic services, but more determined steps to re-establish the faith were taken when in 1858 a site on Coltsgate Hill was bought for the erection of a purpose-built Catholic church, presbytery and school.

The money (£5000) came largely from the Vavasour family of Hazlewood Castle near Tadcaster, and Father Philip Vavasour was to be the first priest. The foundation stone was laid in 1860 and the new church opened two years later - Joseph Hansom was the architect and its curious design must have been much commented on at the time. Officially in the Lombardo Early Decorated Style, the lofty tower unusually is at the altar end of the church, and stands over an apsidal sanctuary. It has been dryly suggested that this back-to-front approach had already been tested by Hansom in the design of his cabs, where the driver sat at the back behind the passengers.

There is much ornate decoration inside, with generous use of marble, and there are striking portraits of saints in mosaic. The elaborate reredos (by Edward Pugin) has sculpted scenes from the life of St. Wilfrid in high relief, and Canon Vavasour is commemorated in a window erected above the high altar in 1888. A later priest, Father de Vacht, carried out a census in 1905 which showed that the Catholic flock at that time totalled 383 souls with 98 children on the school register (the school had opened in 1863). By then the church had gained a prestigious patron in the Marquess of Ripon, a recent convert and posthumous donor of stained glass from his private chapel; appropriately, his burial service was held there in 1909. At the time of the First World War its priest, Father Levick, won widespread recognition (even from the post-war Belgian government) for the help and comfort that he gave to Belgian refugees in the area.

Since then many decades have passed, and St. Wilfrid's church today continues to enjoy a high rating in the popularity stakes.

# The College of Higher Education

### Years of service end in closure

The closure of the Ripon Campus of the University College of Ripon and York St John in 2001 was not the first great change to affect the cause of education on this site - from its opening in 1862; the College underwent major changes at periodic intervals.

The College was built by the Church of England to train women teachers for Elementary Schools. Some years earlier, in 1846, such a college had opened in York, to serve the York and Ripon Dioceses, but the premises proved very inadequate and the move to purpose-built accommodation in Ripon soon followed. The new building could house 63 students; it opened with a mere 32, but by 1867 the total had risen to 57. At the outset the college consisted of little more than the central block - even the chapel was not added for over 30 years.

George Sheffield, the first Principal, unfortunately died almost immediately, but his replacement, the Revd (later Canon) Baynes Badcock stayed in post for 28 years. During those years, the students' life was strictly regimented. They rose at 6.00 am and followed a fixed timetable of lessons and meal-times until 8.30 pm. Diet was dominated by beef, mutton and potatoes (home-grown); there were heavy suet puddings, cakes and fruit pies. Bread was usually home-made. Every Sunday, in their bonnets, jackets and heavy skirts, they walked in crocodile to Holy Trinity church in the morning and to the Cathedral in the afternoon.

The staff consisted of a Lady Superintendent and three Governesses - the Principal lived out. The students' 'Practising School' was Holy Trinity but soon the Cathedral schools (Boys' and Girls') began to be used too. The College was of course subject to regular visits by

Her Majesty's inspectors, the OFSTED equivalent of those days. Revd Badcock retired in 1891, his daughter Mary having years earlier attracted the attention of Charles Dodgson who sent her photograph to John Tenniel as a model for his drawings of Alice.

The next Principal was the 30-year old Revd George Garrod, and the strict rules were slackened a little. Hockey and tennis were introduced, there were many excursions, and students (in pairs) were allowed into town without a governess. By 1908, when Garrod was moved to another church post, there were 141 students, and teaching practice had been widened to include schools in Leeds, Harrogate and Bradford. In 1899 the College had gained its own chapel, with fine stained glass windows, and in 1903 St. Margaret's Lodge was added as the Principal's residence.

Through the 20thC the College expanded in fits and starts in response to changing government education policy. An East Wing was added in 1904, but then demolished in 1930 owing to subsidence problems; at the same time a new West Wing was added, creating the now familiar arches-and-courtyard effect. The dining hall and kitchens were built in the early 1950s, the Hall, Chapel, Harewood Hostel and the Union building in the 1960s. Highfield – formerly the Kearsleys' mansion - was acquired, as well as the former Girls' High School and the cottages on Coltsgate Hill. By the late 1970s, this physical growth, together with soaring numbers (now including men students), a merger with St. John's College York, the offer of B. Ed. Degrees and even non-teaching qualifications, meant that the College had changed out of all recognition. More was to follow however: the greatest change of all was to come when the decision was taken to reduce College costs by closing the Ripon campus (2001). Since then the future of the site and its buildings has remained uncertain, but clearly much is to be given over to housing.

# T. & R. Williamson - Part I

### A notable industry and a colourful personality

In the 19thC Ripon was as famous for varnish making as it had been in previous centuries for making cloth and spurs, and much of that Victorian varnish was produced by the firm of T. & R. Williamson Ltd. Varnish making began in Ripon as a family business founded by a certain Daniel Williamson, a banker who, according to tradition, was attracted to varnish making in 1775 by receiving trade secrets from a grateful French Huguenot refugee whom he had befriended. The new business was set up on the north bank of the Skell downstream from Borrage Bridge where it was to remain for over 200 years.

Daniel died in 1796 aged 72, and the business passed to his grandson (?) Robert. who also combined it with banking. When he eventually died, over 30 years later in 1829, he was succeeded by his son William who again retained his banking interests. William became Mayor in 1847-8 and his business partner Thomas, his half-brother, was Mayor the following year. When William died in 1857 his place in the business was taken by Thomas' son, another Robert, and it was these two who gave their initials to the name of the firm from that time onwards.

In 1867 Thomas died at the Williamson family home of Borrage House, leaving Robert, then aged 42, in charge of the business. His home was at Sunny Bank, further along Borrage Lane; he and his wife Elizabeth had two sons - the elder died at 30, leaving his younger brother Tom as heir to the family estate.

Tom Williamson had an interesting career by any standard, and was fortunate to have it written up by his widow Alice after his death. Born in 1853, he was educated at Ripon Grammar School, Rugby and Oxford, but then decided that his best prospects lay abroad. In 1879 he bought a ranch in the Wild West state of Colorado USA and spent most of the next eight years there. It was not until the early 1890s that he settled again in Ripon, marrying Alice Stevenson. They lived in South Crescent for five years before moving in 1898 to Borrage House, his grandfather's former home.

By that time Tom Williamson had become a Councillor (1895) and was heavily involved in local affairs. Having missed the Millenary Festival of 1886 through being abroad, he played a full role in the 1896 sequel event, the 'Boadicea to Victoria' pageant. Later that year he succeeded the Marquess of Ripon as Mayor (1896/7), the highlights of his term of office being the opening of Queen Victoria's Diamond Jubilee Clock Tower and the planting of twelve lime trees in the Market Place, each by a surviving former Mayor.

In 1894 T. & R. Williamson had become a limited company, with Tom and his father Robert as two of the three directors, but the father remained the dominant figure until his death in 1906. By that time Tom was writing articles for the *Leeds Mercury* and pursuing other interests in music and drama. An energetic managing director was needed to lead the business forward and T.F. Spence was appointed to the post. Most of the remaining years of Tom's life were dominated by the First World War and its impact on Ripon. He died at Borrage House in 1920, aged 67, and his striking memorial (with obelisk) can be seen in the Cathedral churchyard close to Low St. Agnesgate.

# T. & R. Williamson - Part II

## Seeking new markets

As previously noted, Williamson's paint and varnish business was founded in Ripon about 1775 when a banker Daniel Williamson is reputed to have been given trade secrets of varnish-making by a grateful French refugee whom he had befriended. Documents reveal that as early as 1805-10 the new business was sending out travelling representatives to many towns in the north of England, including Leeds, Bradford, Skipton, Preston, Lancaster and Liverpool. Their mission was to seek orders and arrange payments, and their transactions were recorded in diaries which still survive. Carrier services delivered the varnish in copper containers to their customers, mostly local painters.

Apart from domestic use, Williamson's paint and varnish was used in the early 19thC to decorate and protect the bodywork of stage coaches, private carriages and even sedan chairs. In addition to linseed oil, the manufacturing process required imported materials including turpentine and resin (gum) from Virginia and Central Africa respectively. In later years shellac gum was imported from Burma.

The coming of the railways opened up an enormous new market, as their carriages needed both weather-proofing and emblazoning with their company's livery. Much the same was to happen again in later years when trams, charabancs, buses, lorries and cars were coming into general use. Two World Wars brought other requirements such as varnish for shell cases and wooden propellers, and camouflage paint for army vehicles - even as early as 1894 T. & R.Williamson was describing itself as 'Contractors to H.M.'s Government'.

Early 20thC prosperity for the company was reflected in the expansion of its premises along the Skell (see photograph). Despite the presence in Ripon of at least three other varnish manufacturers, Williamsons felt able in 1925 to construct a large and impressive office block close to Borrage Bridge, advertising its presence to all road users. Expansion however could also bring problems - a request to buy a parcel of land from Jepson's Hospital in 1926 in order to consolidate Williamson's holdings led to a sharp refusal, the issue being only resolved when the Bluecoat school closed the following year for financial reasons.

The House of Williamson celebrated its 200th anniversary in 1975 but times were changing. Its local rivals had already gone and there was a move in the industry towards consolidation into larger units. Soon Williamsons itself was caught up in this process, and its new owners decided on a clean start. Although the family name was retained, new premises were built in the 1980s in Stonebridgegate, and the former buildings along the Skell gave way to the impressive housing development to be seen there today. Only the 1925 office block remains, now converted to residential use.

T. & R. Williamson Ltd. is still a leading supplier of specialist paints, and proudly claims to be the oldest established Varnish House in the United Kingdom. It is gratifying that one of Ripon's renowned former industries, with a fascinating history, still survives and flourishes in the City.

# Kearsley's Varnish Works

## Competition for Williamson's

Victorian England was renowned for successful self-made business men, and Ripon itself was not without striking examples. None were more famous in their day than those provided by the House of Kearsley, which in the second half of the 19thC made a major contribution to local government in the town as well as to its economy.

The fortunes of the Kearsley family were laid by one George Kearsley, a coal and iron merchant whose works yard was on the banks of the Skell at Bondgate Green. His business is documented in 1811 and continued until his death aged 71 in 1847. The coal no doubt arrived via the canal, but the advent of the railway shortly after George's death soon made canal-borne coal unprofitable.

George and his wife Elizabeth had seven sons, the youngest of whom was Robert Kearsley, born in 1822 and educated at the Grammar School. After school he joined his father's business which he later took over and developed into a large and successful paint and varnish works (R. Kearsley & Co.), offering serious competition for T. & R. Williamson Ltd. Kearsley himself travelled widely throughout the country securing new orders for his products.

Matters of business inevitably gave him an interest in how the city was governed and, having become a Councillor in 1855, he went on to hold the office of Mayor twice while still in his late thirties (1857-8, 1858-9). Among the civic highlights of

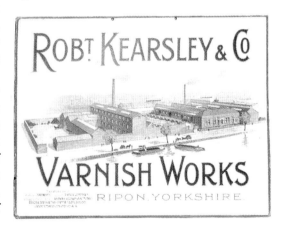

those two years were the acquisition of the Mayor's Chain and Badge, the presentation of the Town Hall clock, and the setting up of a Russian cannon in the Market Place as a victory trophy of the Crimean war.

Having left office, Kearsley was made an Alderman, but now saw a parliamentary career beckoning, and in 1865 briefly became one of Ripon's two M.P.s. He was also a magistrate, an officer of the Ripon Volunteer Corps, and Deputy Lieutenant of the West Riding - a distinguished public servant.

In the early 1860s he had *Highfield* built, a striking Victorian mansion with ambitious architectural features, set next to the College in spacious grounds off Palace Road, where he and his wife Sarah lived with their children and servants. Sarah died in 1891, and when Kearsley himself died the following year, his funeral procession to the Cathedral constituted a major public event.

Their eldest daughter Emily married into the Oxley family and had a number of children, but in 1898 she died at an early age, to be commemorated on the elaborate monument to be seen under the south-west tower of the cathedral. The Kearsleys' son, Harry, 38 at his father's death, sold off the family villa which was to change hands a number of times before being acquired by Ripon College in 1946. When, over fifty years later, the College closed, this elegant Listed building continued briefly as a short course and conference centre.

## Kearsley's Iron Works

### Award-winning agricultural machinery

Robert Kearsley, the varnish manufacturer of Bondgate Green and builder of the ornate mansion off Palace Road known as Highfield, was twice Mayor of Ripon in the 1850s and briefly its M.P.

Robert however had an elder brother Henry, and he too was to make his mark locally and in style. Born in 1812, the fourth son of George Kearsley the Bondgate Green coal merchant, Henry took over the business after his father's death in 1847. But by the 1850s, canal-borne coal was facing fierce competition from rail-borne coal, stockpiled on Ure Bank, and the Kearsley coal business in Bondgate went into terminal decline.

While Henry's brother Robert successfully redeveloped the site into a varnish works, Henry himself turned to iron, and by 1857 he was running an iron foundry off North Street (where the telephone exchange now stands). There his business seems to have gone from strength to strength, eventually employing about 100 operatives, its speciality being the production of reaping and mowing machines, many of which went for export. 'Kearsley's No. 4' became known around the world and his reapers won exhibition awards in many countries. Storing the completed machines became a problem, and led Kearsley to build a huge warehouse off Trinity Lane which then had to be immediately rebuilt after gale damage in 1860.

Kearsley's entry in a trade directory of 1861 provides clear evidence of his not inconsiderable pride in his achievement. While most business entries took up one line, Kearsley claimed a whole paragraph and it is worth quoting in full:

> Henry Kearsley, bar iron merchant, engine builder, iron and brass founder, millwright, manufacturer of the Yorkshire reaping machine & Wardell's side delivery self-acting reaping machine, the patent Buckeye mowing machine & combined mowing and reaping machine, also Spight's patent horse hoe, brick and tile machines, & presses & agricultural implement maker; stoves, grates, kitcheners & weighing machines of every description; works and office, North Street; & depot Trinity Lane.

By 1861 Kearsley had married Jane McIntosh and become a Ripon councillor, and was so highly regarded that he was elected to serve three terms of office as Mayor (1871-4). Perhaps the highlights of his mayoralty were officially greeting the soon-to-be Marquess of Ripon on his return from a successful diplomatic mission to America, and taking part in civic celebrations to mark the completion of Sir George Gilbert Scott's lengthy restoration works at the Cathedral. When Kearsley died in 1876 he was buried in the cathedral churchyard.

Not long before his death he had taken his nephew George (to be Mayor 1881-2) into the business, and by 1895 it had become the British Iron and Implement Works. References to it finally cease in the 1930s - was it a victim of the Great Depression? The large warehouse in Trinity Lane still survives (now North Yorkshire Timber Co. Ltd) but there is little trace of the foundry and workshop buildings off North Street which for years had been the home of one of Ripon's most renowned business enterprises. The 20thC was also to see the demise of the Kearsley family itself, formerly one of Ripon's great Victorian dynasties.


# The Girls' Home in Bondgate

## Victorian concern for orphans

People today will seek in vain for this large and impressive building in Bondgate, but for over sixty years the Ripon Home for Girls was a familiar part of the local townscape - on the west side of the main road, a little south of the junction with Mawson Lane.

HOME FOR GIRLS, BONDGATE, RIPON.

Its origin lay in Victorian concern for poor children in need of help - in this case girls who had been orphaned - and the lead was appropriately taken by the aptly named Dean Goode, who founded the home in 1862 as the Ripon Industrial Home for Girls. Its purpose was to "befriend poor girls of good character, more especially those that are motherless.....by training them in habits of industry, giving them instruction calculated to fit them for domestic service or as mother of a household of their own, and securing to them religious teaching.".

Funds were raised by subscription to purchase the existing building (plus its two acres of land) and several extensions were added later. In its heyday it had a dining room, kitchen, wash-house, laundry, bathroom, dormitories and schoolroom.

It had 13 girls on opening, but by the end of the century the average number was 25-30. We are fortunate in that life in the Girls' Home in Edwardian times was vividly recorded for posterity by Alice Collier who was there for ten years from the age of five. Her fascinating account of her experiences (*Alice's Story*) was published by the Civic Society in 1991 and is still available in the shops. Alice was separated from her five brothers and sisters when her mother died in 1909 at the age of 29. They had lived in Scarborough, but the children were then dispersed, and Alice was sent to the orphanage at Ripon.

The girls went to bed early and got up early to a breakfast of lumpy porridge, but with bread and margarine on Sundays and a mug of cocoa. There was meat for dinner followed by milk or suet pudding, and for tea there was a slice of bread and dripping or jam (home-made from their own fruit trees). There was always a turkey for Christmas. The girls made their own bread, 20 loaves at a time, getting the yeast from nearby Hepworth's Brewery. To ward off sickness they were given brimstone and treacle.

A private chaplain gave weekly instruction in scripture, and the girls served as the choir for St. Mary Magdalen's Chapel in Stonebridgegate, proceeding there on a Sunday morning in their boaters and navy blue capes in the inevitable crocodile. They then attended afternoon service at the Cathedral, which once a month took the form of a special children's service, and finally there was evening service at St. Johns......! For entertainment there were walks along the Skell and Ure, and silent films on a Saturday at the Palladium (Kirkgate).

The home had its own schoolroom, but standards may not have been high since in 1913 it was decided that the girls should instead attend the Cathedral School. Household management was learned back in the Home however, and the girls went out on domestic service work-placements before leaving at fifteen. In 1927, a few years after Alice left, the Home gave up its premises in Bondgate and moved to West Mount, off College Road, where ten years later it merged with Dr. Barnardo's. Back in Bondgate, the original building was requisitioned by the War Department during World War II, and then demolished in 1946.

# The *King's Arms*

## Drastic change comes to Bedern Bank

A property boarded up, awaiting demolition, is always a sad sight, especially if, as in this case, it had once been a place of enjoyment and entertainment. The *King's Arms* pub stood at the foot of Bedern Bank, close to the junction with Skellgarths, and had been there for many years when this photograph was taken in the late 1950s.

The building suggests an 18thC date, but it is first recorded as a tavern in 1822. For much of the 19C it was run by the Gearman family, but by 1897 the proprietor was David Castle, and a vivid account survives of his hostelry as it was four years later in 1901. It was then owned by Hepworth & Co., the Bondgate brewers nearby, and catered above all for 'stand-up' beer drinkers who liked to have their elbow on the bar in the tap room. Food was not normally on offer, and visitor accommodation was limited to one bedroom. The only toilet was out in the yard, but "clean and in good condition".

David Castle was still in charge there when the Great War began, and one wonders how these facilities coped with the huge surge in trade which came when first navvies and then thirsty soldiers from the Army Camp descended on the town in large numbers.

By the late 1930s, however, circumstances had changed dramatically since he decision had been taken by the Ministry of Transport and the County Council to ease the city's traffic problems by driving a Ripon Relief Road up a widened Bedern Bank. Although years later this ill-advised scheme was rightly abandoned, it was too late for the *King's Arms* and much of the neighbouring property, the demolition of which had begun in the late 1950s despite vigorous local opposition. For years to follow, the western side of Bedern Bank was a featureless open space used as a car park until the present housing was eventually built, but in between times an archaeological dig had at

least established that the original medieval Bedern (the College of the Vicars' Choral) had not been on this side of the road.

However, a hidden feature that had lain close to the *King's Arms* in its heyday was the stone-walled medieval mill-race that ran down Skellgarths from Water Skellgate, serving Union Mill near the present day roundabout before debouching into the Skell. Still an open water course in 1800, it was vaulted over in the 19C, but then went out of use by 1900 with the demise of the mills. Later it was occasionally broken into by accident, giving rise no doubt to the legend of a tunnel to Fountains Abbey.

The *King's Arms*, probably originally dedicated to King George III, was of course one of many pub casualties to occur in Ripon during the 20C. Others in that part of town included the *Bricksetters' Arms* in Bondgate, the *Brewers' Arms* by Bondgate Green Bridge, and the *Horse and Jockey* in Skellgarths (where the Library later stood).

## King Street and Wellington Street

### When stone gave way to iron

This rare and attractive watercolour of Bondgate Bridge with the Cathedral beyond was painted in about 1850. It contains a lot of interest, including a depiction of St. John's Chapel before it was rebuilt (1868), and shows the stone version of Bondgate Bridge that was to be superseded by the present iron structure in 1892, unfortunately now seriously weakened.

People crossing the bridge northwards in mid-Victorian times entered King Street as they do today, but there were then terraced houses on both sides of the road; those on the east side were demolished a hundred years later, their position now marked by the electricity sub-station. At the northern end of the street stood the Bedern Bank corn mill, a church property since medieval times but disused by 1900. In 1914 the Church gave the land to the city as a children's playground, and as such it still happily flourishes today.

Among the traders in King Street in 1901, as recorded in the Directory of that year, were a milk dealer, two grocers and Benson's the ironmonger (soon to relocate to the Old Market Place). There was also the *Bottle and Jug*, John Park's off-licence. In 1895, one of the street's residents, a 68-year-old widow, had suffered a bizarre death, having been found drowned - head first - down a peggy tub with surprisingly little water in it. At the inquest it was deemed an accident.

Running off King Street at right angles to the west was Wellington Street, which suddenly appears on the map in 1818 and presumably was laid out to honour the name of the victor of Waterloo (1815). Designed as a cul-de-sac, perhaps to provide more terraced housing, it had by 1854 the Wellington Street Brewery on its north side, and Bondgate Brewery to the south, immediately across the river near the bridge - leaving the Wellington Street residents an interesting choice of aromas to savour!

In 1901, with the two large Skell Villas having arrived at its west end, the street included a dressmaker, a cabinet maker and a wool merchant. Since the mid-19C a branch of the Severs family had been operating a fellmonger's and wool merchant's business there. By 1901 the business had passed to John Severs and Son at No.14, and it was he who years before (1875), with great public spiritedness, had paid for a horse and cattle fountain to be erected at the town end of North Bridge. Severs' name can still be read on the fountain, now in Spa Park, to which it was transferred in the late 1920s, by which time petrol had become more in demand than water. The wool merchant's business later passed to Frederick Trees (Mayor 1938-9) and from him to his elder son.

As with Bedern Bank, it was the proposed Ring Road that was to have dire effects on the neighbourhood, precipitating the destruction in the 1960s of the terraced houses on the east side of King Street, although the proposed relief road would have swept up Bondgate Green Lane and Boroughbridge Road before turning up Bedern Bank. Certainly King Street lost its character as an enclosed street, but perhaps the west-side residents gained a better view of the play park and the river!

# Ripon Clockmakers

## Craftsmen with time on their hands

Ripon has long been famous for its craftsmen, particularly its spur makers, but in the 18th and 19th centuries the town also produced its fair share of clock and watchmakers.

This was the golden age of the grandfather or more properly the longcase clock, built in mahogany, oak or walnut in a variety of styles, with brass or painted dials, 30 hour or 8 day movements, and all the familiar accessories of weights, pendulums and decorative spandrels. Some even gave the day's date and the phases of the moon.

After Thomas Tompion in the late 17C demonstrated what handsome items of furniture longcase clocks could be, they enjoyed much popularity and clockmakers were able to take full advantage of this new public taste. Clockmakers put together 'the works' whilst the wooden cases were constructed by cabinet makers.

One of the earliest recorded clockmakers in Ripon was George Mills, who provided a new clock in the Minster Church in 1724. Minster clocks are a story in themselves: within a century Mills' clock had been replaced (1809) by one made by Thwaites of London, set in the south-west tower with an external dial. This in turn was replaced in 1906 by a clock made by Potts of Leeds and Newcastle, this time with two external dials (facing south as well as west).

Later in the 18C John Gilbertson, father and son, were active clockmakers, operating from their workshop in the Market Place (now Thomas the Baker). Gilbertson senior, a member of Ripon Corporation, produced longcase clocks for thirty years until his death in 1793, and a fine example of his work may still be seen in the Spa Hotel. In a rather bizarre incident Gilbertson had earlier (1777) made a minor fortune for himself when he was appointed one of the government agents responsible for collecting defective gold coins. He bought a property in Sharow from the proceeds which became known as Light Guinea Hall.

A clock and watchmaker who became Mayor was Richard Johnson, who held the office in 1814/15 and again in 1825/6. The work obviously suited his health since he lived to be 85 and was practising his trade until only a few years before his death. Years later, his Market Place premises are now occupied by Jon Barrie.

Another clock and watch maker to achieve the mayoralty was Willey Carter, who held office in 1817/18 and again in 1829/30. Carter was a jeweller too and eventually handed over the business to his son Henry. Like Richard Johnson, Carter survived into his eighties, as did his son after him. Their one-time workshop in the Square is now Appleton's.

Yet another local clock and watch maker to achieve fame did so by a different route. Richard Blakeborough in 1859 provided the illuminated clock for the pediment of the Town Hall which people still find useful today. Blakeborough also produced longcase clocks, maintaining what had become by mid-Victorian times a long-established Ripon craft, although few examples survive to the present day.

# The Ripon Maze

### Intricate and intriguing

Not the least interesting of Ripon's 'Ancient Charms', but one that has long disappeared, was its original Maze, which was drawn and recorded in the early 19C. Known as the Maiden's Bower, it was to be found off what is now Palace

Road, set back on the north side nearly opposite the present day Primrose estate. Its location was then part of Ripon's High Common, and it was the enclosure of that Common which led to the unfortunate and needless destruction of the Maze by ploughing in 1827.

Its end is better documented than its origin, which is shrouded in mystery, but it could have been there for centuries. It bore no resemblance to the Cretan Labyrinth (famous for its passages and Minotaur), nor was it the familiar tall

hedge maze (as at Hampton Court) where people enjoy getting lost - a type that was added to ornamental gardens from Tudor times onwards. The much simpler and more common form of maze, to which the Ripon example belonged, had turf walls only a few inches high, but those walls still created a very intricate and fascinating pattern and enclosed a very special central space.

Some examples of this earlier form of maze are thought to date back to pre-Christian times, and were traditionally associated with fertility customs and countryside lore. Turf mazes came to enjoy special popularity in late medieval times when they were deemed to be sacred sites incorporating Christian symbolism and were depicted even in some churches, but one suspects they were always more appreciated for their fun value than for ritual purposes. The centre of the maze was a magical spot where, at Midsummer, children could "kneel down and hear the fairies singing".

The date when the Ripon example was constructed may not be known, but the local antiquary Tuting recorded that it had a diameter of 20 yards. There was a similar maze at Asenby, near Topcliffe, that could still be traced in 1908.

Although Ripon's original maze has been lost, its design has been preserved, and so it has been possible for the Rotary Club of Ripon Rowels to recreate it in Spa Park, as an intriguing source of wonder for children of all ages.

# The Temple Garden

### A haven of peace near the town centre

Some workers or visitors looking for a place in the sun to eat their lunch, or just to sit and relax, seek out the Temple Garden off Allhallowgate, one of Ripon's pocket parks that has particular charm. But the Temple Garden was created only in quite recent times (1986).

Before then the earliest use of this elongated plot of land so far discovered was as a chapel with burial ground, founded in 1818 by a Nonconformist group called

Independents, and their Temple chapel stood at the north end of the site. Over a hundred strong, with their own minister, they flourished here for more than half a century until in 1871, now part of the Congregationalist movement, they moved to the new church that had just been built in North Road (today the site of the flats opposite the Police Station). Perhaps one advantage of this move was to get away from the noise emanating from Kearsley's Iron Foundry (where the telephone exchange now stands).

Their previous home was regrettably abandoned; in the 1890s the Temple structure was removed but the gravestones remained, an ongoing reminder that former worshippers here had included the Sutcliffes, the Wrays, the Barkers, the Gambages, the Walkers, the Peacocks, the Blackburns and the Shields. These memorial stones, many of young people, are now set against the perimeter wall, their inscriptions steadily eroding.

Ripon City Council took on responsibility for the site in 1919, but by the time the gravestones were rearranged in the 1960s to facilitate grass cutting, the neglected northern end of the plot had become a major eyesore and dumping ground. Clean-ups by volunteers in the late 1960s and 1970s only brought temporary relief to the problem and no real progress was made until in the early 1980s Ripon Environment Committee negotiated with Harrogate Borough

Council for the site (referred to then as the Dissenters' Graveyard) to be turned into a public garden via a Manpower Services Commission Project.

The work was completed very successfully and in the Festival Year of 1986 the re-styled 'Temple Garden' was formally opened by TV gardener Geoffrey Smith. Since then the grass has been cut by Harrogate Council, whilst all other matters have been overseen by a Temple Garden Management Committee (1988) which has employed a gardener and held fund-raising events, in particular the annual springtime open-air Lunch. Contributions from the City Council and various voluntary groups have helped to cover maintenance costs, and further improvements, including an access route to North Street, were undertaken in the 1990s, funded through the Civic Trust Ripon Project.

In the spring of 2001 Harrogate Borough Council agreed to accept responsibility for all maintenance work and take the entire Garden into its care in order to guarantee its future as a public recreational area.

# Allhallows Park

## Reclaimed from a wasteland

Allhallows Park, next to the three-level car park east of the Market Place, has become a familiar sight to many people since it was created by the Civic Society in 1991. It offers a children's playground, seats for rest and recuperation, and a very pleasant short-cut to the town centre for east-side residents. But as late as the 1980s, it was a wilderness and tip.

The steep slope of the ground stems from the fact that most of the site was once part of Allhallows Hill, the remainder of which provides gardens for the residents of Victoria Grove. In medieval times there may have been a chapel on the hill and many burials have been discovered there, one in quite recent times.

The hill itself is a huge natural mound of gravel left behind at the end of the Ice Age, and this made it a tempting source of cobbles for builders in past centuries. As a result probably more than half the hill has been quarried away, leaving what remains as an imposing back-drop to the terraced park.

To the north the park is enclosed by the cottages that lie along lower Allhallowgate, a street that is recorded as early as the 13C and is probably much older, since it links to St. Marygate, Stonebridgegate and Priest Lane, close to where Ripon's monastic origins lay. In one of the cottages, the artist and entertainer Jim Gott lived as a boy.

Near the park, on St. Marygate, is the block of flats that some years ago replaced a line of old cottages stretching along the street, several of which still survive further along

opposite the one-time House of Correction. On the very corner of St. Marygate and Allhallowgate stood the *Fleece Inn*, recorded from 1822 onwards, but the building itself is probably 18C. A report on licensed houses in 1901 showed that the *Fleece* was then owned by Hepworth's brewery of Bondgate. The licensee was George Marston, the pub offered only a stand-up bar, there were three stalls for horses but no accommodation for visitors. Light refreshments were available, particularly at race times, when the *Fleece* found itself on one of the prime routes from the railway station to the racecourse. It has now been converted to residential use but its outer wall still incorporate one of Ripon's few surviving Victorian letter boxes.

Vaux Brewery, who owned the *Fleece* in its final years, also owned the land behind it, once an orchard but by the 1980s a neglected wasteland, and it was their decision to sell it cheaply to the Civic Society that made possible the creation of Allhallows Park in 1991. In 1999 with grant aid the playground was upgraded and re-equipped, allowing the whole park to be transferred to Harrogate Borough Council, who now maintain it for public use.

# Thomas Gent

### The gold and the dross

Thomas Gent, 18C antiquarian and printer, was a mixed blessing for Ripon. On the one hand he has left us the earliest known History of Ripon, containing a map full of interesting detail - yet on the other hand he launched a fable that has been repeated ever since, namely that Ripon received a charter from

Alfred the Great in 886. Any student of that period knows that King Alfred of Wessex had no jurisdiction in the north of England, and in 886 moreover was recovering from a fierce struggle for survival with a Viking army, facts that Gent chose to overlook.

However, Gent's book and map are a fascinating source of information. He spent most of his life in York where he had a printer's workshop in Coffee Yard off Stonegate, and it was there that his *History of the Loyal Town of Rippon* was published in 1733 (naturally he also wrote a history of York). He died in poverty in 1778 aged 87. The map is of special interest. The impressive panoramic view at the top not only shows birds of prodigious size circling the collegiate church, but also the Obelisk (then recently erected), the Skell, and Borrage bridge. The depiction in a roundel of the ribboned Horn shows that it symbolised Ripon even in those days, whilst the seal of St. Wilfrid in a similar roundel confirms the saint's age-old importance to the town.

The street names set out below the roundels make familiar reading with odd exceptions: North Street was then *The Horse-fair* and Coltsgate Hill had changed breed to *Cowsgate Hill*! Bedern Bank was apparently *Betharon Bank* and St Agnesgate was *Anna's Gate*. *School Lane* (South Walk) is a reminder of the early location of the Grammar School, whilst *Goose Common* has been reinstated in our own time opposite the Clock Tower. Note the nearby pinfold (*★*) in the middle of the road which was no doubt responsible for the original traffic problems in this area.

Also of interest are the references to Ripon's ancient monastic sites: the original pre-Wilfridian Celtic Monastery off Priest Lane (now Ripon House), and the Benedictine (?) monastery behind Huby's Wall in St. Marygate, where a pre-Conquest chapel was located by archaeologists in the 1950s. Also marked are Ripon's three well-known medieval hospitals, as well as Jepson's Bluecoat charity school. Finally, note the route of the medieval mill race, flowing in from the west and first marked where the Hugh Ripley Hall now is. Long before the Alma Weir was constructed, this extraordinarily long waterway traversed the town and the gardens of High St Agnesgate before finally returning its water to the Skell on the eastern edge of Ripon at Low Mill.

Ripon is fortunate to have such a detailed map from so early a date.


# Captain John Elliott

### He sailed with Captain Cook

Ripon's army connection is well known, but its naval connection less so. This is unfortunate, since it centres on one of the finest Georgian houses in the city, originally called Elliott House but now known as Holmefield House, on the road to Harrogate. Despite alterations to the windows and division into flats, it is still much as it was built in the late 1780s when it became the residence of Lieutenant John Elliott, a commander in the Royal Navy.

At that time Elliott, born in 1759, was a famous seafarer who as a very young man had served as a midshipman on the *Resolution*, the ship which Captain Cook

commanded on the voyage of exploration that took him round the world in the years from 1772 to 1775. Sailing south from Plymouth, the Resolution reached the South Atlantic and dodging the icebergs, crossed the Antarctic Circle in January 1773. At the end of that year Cook set off again, this time south of New Zealand, exploring previously uncharted waters. After a year in the South Pacific the *Resolution* headed home in November 1774, rounding Cape Horn and returning via the Atlantic. For the young John Elliott this must have been the experience of a lifetime.

At that time Britain was about to be plunged into war with her American colonies, who soon had the active support of France under Louis XVI, anxious to recover losses suffered earlier in the century. In 1782 the future of Britain's possessions in the West Indies was at stake when Admiral Rodney's fleet clashed with the French at the so-called Battle of the Saints (named after a local group of islands). The Royal Navy won the battle, but Lieutenant John Elliott, now commander of the *Ajax* (74 guns), was severely wounded, and this seems to have ended his active naval career.

The Navy's loss however was Ripon's gain, since by the close of the 1780s he had built Elliott House, and with his wife Isabella was about to embark on creating a large family (clearly unaffected by his war wound). Babies came thick and fast - Sibella (1789), Charles (1790), William (1792), Gilbert (1795), Jane (1796), Maria (1797), Margaretta (1799), Louisa (1801), Anna Maria (1802), Charlotte (1803), and Frederick (1808). Tragically however most of them died young, not just in infancy but also in their teens. In 1821 the family vault in the Minster church was declared to be full.

Captain Elliott also played a leading part in the town's social life, and in 1823 is recorded as helping to publicise a season of balls at the Assembly Rooms (now the Town Hall). He died in 1834 at the age of 75, "greatly respected for his strict integrity and uprightness" and his personal details are given at length on a memorial stone in the south nave aisle of the Cathedral. A few years later (1841) his widow Isabella died, aged 78. It proved to be the end of an era for Elliott House.

# J. R. Walbran

## Ripon's premier Victorian historian

If Ripon's historic past is its greatest asset, no one did more to highlight its importance in the 19thC than Ripon's greatest Victorian historian, John Richard Walbran.

His family roots in the city were not deep. His father came from a village near Bedale, but by 1816 had moved to Ripon where he set up as an iron merchant. He was elected a councillor and went on to become twice Mayor (1840-2), but died only a few years later leaving five sons, of whom John Richard was the eldest.

Born in 1817, he was educated at a school in Whixley run by the vicar - a relative of his mother's. He did not go on to university, despite being a natural scholar, but instead entered his father's business as an iron merchant which was run from the family home at Fall Croft, a house that still survives on the corner of Blossomgate and Trinity Lane (creating an awkward pinch-point for drivers). After his father's death the business continued as John Walbran & Co, but in the 1850s he also ran a wine and spirits business in Park Street. How far other members of the family were involved is not clear, but in 1856 Walbran could be described as an 'Iron and Spirit Merchant', a curious combination of trades.

In 1849, when he was 32, he married Jane, daughter of the late town clerk, Richard Nicholson. Shortly afterwards, at the time of the 1851 census, she gave her age as 25, though in a similar census ten years later, she declared herself to be 31, a phenomenon familiar to those who study 19thC census returns. In 1850 he became a local councillor and, like his father before him, went on to become twice Mayor of Ripon (1855-7).

In addition to his family business and council activities, the young Walbran began serious study of local history, and so successfully that in 1854 he was elected a Fellow of the prestigious Society of Antiquaries. What had he done to earn this recognition? Ten years earlier (1844) he had published a "Guide to Ripon and Harrogate" which was very well reviewed and went through many editions in the years to come. But Walbran was also an amateur archaeologist, competent by the standards of his day, and in 1846 he excavated two round barrows near Copt Hewick. But then in the early 1850s, after work at Markenfield Hall, he turned to Fountains Abbey and supervised excavation and conservation work there, following which, after enormous research in libraries, he published some of the abbey's medieval records (*Memorials of Fountains*). The printer of these and all Walbran's other works was his close personal friend William Harrison who had a great love of local history himself and

personally set much of the type. Harrison died in 1867, and within two years his friend Walbran was dead too.

Not least of Walbran's achievements was his study of the Saxon crypt beneath the Cathedral, the age and importance of which was at that time only coming to be recognised. In 1858 he found human bones and other items behind one of the niches, but their date was uncertain.

Walbran's health suffered in the 1860s and he appears to have had a stroke in 1868, dying at his home Fall Croft in April the following year at the early age of 51. He was buried across the road in Holy Trinity churchyard.

# Bishop Stubbs

## Scholar and churchman with local roots

In July 1874 that prestigious body the Royal Archaeological Institute held its conference in Ripon, and a large company of archaeologists spent several days listening to addresses and touring historic buildings in the locality. The address one evening was given by Professor William Stubbs, one of the most highly regarded historians of his day, and an old boy of Ripon Grammar School.

Stubbs had been born in 1825, the eldest of six children of a Knaresborough solicitor and the grandson of a wealthy wine merchant in Boroughbridge. Perhaps through family connections with the Oxley family young William was sent to Ripon rather than Knaresborough Grammar School, and so came to know Dr. Longley who, in 1836, became the first Bishop of Ripon. Over the years Longley, who went on to become Archbishop of Canterbury, was able to help William Stubbs' career on several occasions, initially in the early 1840s when Stubbs was awarded an undergraduate place at Christchurch College Oxford. There he set about the serious study of history, aided by an apparently "amazing" memory.

For a career, however, he turned to the Church of England and in 1850 secured the living of Navestock in Essex, where he proved to be a conscientious parish priest with a good sense of humour. At the end of the 1850s he married the village

schoolmistress, and raised a family of five sons and a daughter.

In the early 1860s his career began to take off when his patron Archbishop Longley appointed him Librarian at Lambeth Palace, and Stubbs was able to concentrate on historical research. Again with Longley's help he was appointed Regius Professor of History at Oxford in 1866. Two years later he became Curator of the Bodleian Library.

It was in these years that Stubbs won his reputation as one of the country's leading historians specialising in constitutional history, and through this renown he was asked to address the members of the Royal Archaeological Institute in Ripon in 1874. Stubbs' great interest was the development of national and local government in England over the centuries; he argued that the country's much loved traditional liberties stemmed not from Magna Carta but from much earlier Anglo-Saxon times, when Englishmen had much in common with Germans. At the Ripon conference he contented himself with speculation that Ripon was the centre of an ancient unit of administration that pre-dated even Wilfrid's Liberty of the 7thC. No doubt while in Ripon he was also pleased to re-visit the haunts of his school days (when the Grammar School was in High St. Agnesgate).

Perhaps as a result of his historical studies Stubbs developed a passionate interest in genealogy, and after many years' research into his own ancestry he published a detailed study indicating connections with numerous well-known local families.

In 1879 Stubbs became a Canon of St. Paul's and now developed his career in the church, becoming Bishop of Chester in 1884 and then Bishop of Oxford in 1888. He died just over a hundred years ago, aged 75, in 1901. The Grammar School is no doubt proud to have Stubbs as one of their "old boys", but Ripon too should be glad to be linked to one of the great scholars of Queen Victoria's reign.

# The Bishop's Palace

## Built to impress

The very name of Palace Road reminds us that there was once a palace, though not a royal one, on the outskirts of Ripon. Shielded by trees and set back from the road for the sake of privacy, it has never been a familiar landmark in the town, especially perhaps after losing its 'palace' status well over 50 years ago.

It began however as the official residence of the Bishop of Ripon, following the creation of the Diocese of Ripon in 1836, a step taken primarily to ensure that the Anglican Church was able to offer pastoral care to the fast-growing population of industrial Leeds. The diocese was carved out of the existing sprawling dioceses of York and Chester, with Ripon remaining part of the Archdiocese of York. It was only at this stage, in comparatively recent times, that Ripon Minster, the age-old collegiate church, became a Cathedral and the town could claim city status.

The first Bishop of Ripon was Dr. Charles Longley, an illustrious cleric who at an early stage in his career was headmaster of Harrow, and later became Bishop of Durham, Archbishop of York and finally

Archbishop of Canterbury. He received the warm congratulations of Ripon Corporation in November 1836 and preached his first sermon the following month, well reviewed by the *Leeds Mercury*, but he had to wait some time for his official residence to be constructed. The necessary land (over 100 acres) had first to be obtained from Elizabeth Sophia Lawrence of Studley Royal, who also provided the building stone, after which the new Bishop laid the foundation stone in October 1838 at what was inevitably a great civic occasion (ending with the usual junketing).

The palace, built in the Tudor style, was designed by a London architect William Railton, who then went off to design Nelson's Column, and in the autumn of 1841 the Bishop's residence was ready for its incumbent. Initially it had a small private chapel, but this proved inadequate, and in 1846 the Archbishop of York offered the money (£3000) to provide a considerably larger one, primarily for the benefit of the bishop's household and the people of North Lees. Railton was again the architect, and this time he opted for the Perpendicular style, which allowed for the insertion of very large windows.

Its eastern semi-hexagonal apse has colourful stained glass windows representing Christ and the Evangelists (1852). One of them commemorates the work of the Revd Charles Dodgson, Archdeacon of Richmond and a Canon of the Cathedral, but best known as the father of Charles Lutwidge Dodgson, the author Lewis Carroll.

Successive Bishops occupied the Palace for nearly 100 years until in 1940 (at about the same time that the Deans were abandoning the Old Deanery) it was decided to give up the Palace and move to somewhere smaller - High Berrys on Hutton Bank, which has since been known as Bishop Mount.

Barnardo's acquired the former palace and ran it for several decades, until the need for purpose-built accommodation within the grounds led to its being sold into private hands. Although now a private residence, the Chapel still retains its stained glass, oak pews and panelling, and not surprisingly is a Grade II Listed Building.

# The First Marquess of Ripon

## Public servant and local benefactor

A new baby at No.10? Most recently Leo Blair; but once George Frederick Samuel Robinson, born in September 1827, the son of the then Prime Minister, Viscount Goderich. This baby was to grow up to become a leading Liberal politician, a statesman who helped to run Queen Victoria's Empire, a dedicated public servant in his part of Yorkshire, and a local philanthropist in the best tradition of *noblesse oblige*. Ripon was fortunate to have him so close by at Studley Royal.

Although he was born at 10 Downing Street, his weak father 'Goody Goderich' was soon out of office, not to return. The young George Robinson launched his own political career by becoming M.P. for Hull in 1852, then Huddersfield

(1853-7) and then the West Riding (1857-9). Earlier he had married (1851) his cousin Henrietta Vyner, elder daughter of Captain Henry Vyner. On his father's death in 1859 he took his seat in the House of Lords, and later that year succeeded his uncle (Earl de Grey) at Studley Royal.

Being a peer in those days was no hindrance to holding high government office, and he filled a succession of important posts in the 1860s. Favoured by Prime Minister Gladstone he was Lord President of the Council from 1868-73, and during that time he was created first Marquess of Ripon (1871) after negotiating the settlement of a dispute with the U.S.A. When Gladstone again became P.M. in 1880, the Marquess became Viceroy and Governor-General of India, and left his statue behind in Calcutta. This was arguably his most testing post - although he was later First Lord of the Admiralty (1886), Colonial Secretary (1892-5), a Privy Councillor and a Knight of the Garter.

It is amazing that he found time to do anything else, but he also managed at different periods to be Lord Lieutenant of the North Riding, Chairman of the West Riding County Council, Chancellor of the University of Leeds, and Grand Master of the Freemasons of England.

What time did he have for Ripon? Quite a lot, it would seem. In previous articles we have seen how he made land available at Bishopton for the Grammar School to move there, and thirty years later he helped to promote the Ripon Spa project. But his best known act of public generosity was to present the Town Hall to the City Corporation in 1897, shortly after he had been Mayor himself in 1895-6. The Town Hall had been built in 1800 by Elizabeth Allanson as Assembly Rooms, but the Corporation had been allowed to make increasing use of it, so the final transfer of ownership was the logical end to the story. However, there is a twist to the tale: 77 years later ownership of the building was to transfer yet again, this time to Harrogate Borough Council (1974).

Studley Royal

Studley Church, Ripon.

The Marquess caused something of a sensation in 1874 by converting to Roman Catholicism, and St.Wilfrid's on Coltsgate Hill became his church. There his funeral service took place when in 1909 he died at the age of 81, and he was laid to rest in St. Mary's church in Studley Park, where the Marchioness had been buried two years earlier. A few years later another statue of the Marquess was erected - this time in Spa Gardens - and his public offices are proudly listed on the pedestal for all to see today.

# Newby Hall Disasters

### Two traumatic years for the Vyner family

As previously noted, in 1859 Frederick Robinson succeeded to the Earldom of Ripon on his father's death, and in that same year he also inherited the Studley estate and title from his uncle the Earl de Grey. His most prestigious title, however, was to come in 1871 when he was created Marquess of Ripon. By then he had been married 20 years - to his cousin Henrietta Vyner of Newby Hall, daughter of Captain Henry Vyner. The Captain died in 1861, leaving the Newby estate in the hands of his widow Lady Mary Vyner and her family - four sons and two daughters. She was however to need family support badly, since within a few years, by a strange coincidence, tragic events twice brought Newby Hall into the national headlines.

The first occasion was early in February 1869, when the York and Ainsty Hunt, in pursuit of their quarry, needed to cross the swollen river Ure at Newby. The flat-bottomed ferry boat was brought across the river at the request of Sir Charles Slingsby, the Master of the Hunt, and some eleven huntsmen and their horses were crowded on to it. It then set off to cross the river, being drawn on a chain, but before reaching even the half way stage, the horses took fright and panicked, and in the ensuing chaos the boat turned over, trapping men and horses beneath it. Some spectators bravely swam out to help, and lines formed from knotted whips were thrown out. One man clung to the ferry chain and others to the overturned boat, but six men drowned that day, including the Master of the Hunt and the two ferrymen. Nine horses were also lost. Two sons of Lady Vyner were involved, but both escaped with their lives.

In April 1870, just over a year after this disaster, Lady Mary Vyner had further bad news to face. Her third son, 23-year-old Frederick, along with several aristocratic companions, was captured by Greek brigands and held to ransom. One hostage was released to try to raise the money, but the brigands increased the amount to £50,000 when they realised who their prisoners were. However, eleven days later the Greek government sent in troops, and in the ensuing shoot-out four hostages were stabbed to death, Frederick Vyner being the last to die, apparently displaying great courage to the end. The brigands were all killed or captured, but the news caused a sensation and reverberated around Europe. There was a popular outcry in

FREDERICK VYNER

England, the press attacked Greece indiscriminately, and even Queen Victoria joined in the criticism.

Not the least to be distressed by Frederick's death were his sister and brother-in-law, soon to become the first Marquess and Marchioness of Ripon. But the most affected must have been Frederick's sorrowing mother, who used the £25,000 collected for his ransom to build the memorial church of Christ the Consoler in the park at Newby Hall, designed by William Burges in the fashionable Gothic Revival style. One of its windows also commemorates the boat disaster. For Lady Mary, the bad news was not yet over - her second son Reginald, aged only 31, died in September 1870.

## The Second Marquess of Ripon

### At home on the moors

It is well known that the owners of the great house and deer park at Studley Royal had a considerable influence on Ripon's affairs over several centuries, but details of individual members of the family remain a common cause of confusion. Quite apart from mix-ups over John and William Aislabie, there is a tendency among the unwary to merge together the first and second Marquesses of Ripon.

Though father and son, they were very different in character and interests. The first Marquess has already been discussed, and the host of public offices which he held throughout a long and distinguished career can be studied on the pedestal of his statue in Spa Gardens. The second Marquess however was a much more shadowy and private figure, and no statue to him was ever erected.

He was born Frederick Oliver Robinson in 1852, and whilst still in his twenties served as M.P. for Ripon from 1874 to 1880 when Benjamin Disraeli was Prime Minister. In May 1885, now

the Earl de Grey, he married Gladys Lonsdale, the sister of the Earl of Pembroke and Montgomery and already a widow since the death of her first husband, the fourth Earl of Lonsdale. By all accounts they had strongly contrasting personalities, the Earl being humourless and besotted with shooting game, whilst Gladys was outgoing, vivacious and committed to ballet, the opera and London social life.

By common consent Gladys was also extremely good looking. Years later (1913) she was described in the *Ripon Gazette* in these terms: "She has immense personal charm and has grown middle aged without losing her wonderful looks. They have ripened but she is still the handsomest woman of her age in society". She became a close friend of Queen Alexandra.

The Earl meanwhile was concentrating on competitive game shooting and was clearly determined to be seen to be the best shot in the land, keeping detailed records of all his kills, which over the years numbered more than half a million. His victims included pheasants, grouse, partridges, woodcock, snipe, duck, hares, rabbits and red deer. Not all his shooting was done at home - on visits abroad he also bagged rhinos, tigers and other big game.

On the death of his father in 1909 he inherited the title of Marquess of Ripon, whilst Gladys became Marchioness. The following year King Edward died, bringing George V to the throne, and as such he joined shooting parties at Studley Royal in 1911 and 1913. Then came the Great War and a stark change of mood. Gladys now devoted herself to the cause of disabled soldiers, and in her will left money to the Soldiers and Sailors Help Society. She herself died late in the war (1917), and a hospital for disabled soldiers was founded at Roehampton in her memory.

After the war the Marquess continued his shooting pursuits, perfecting (after practice) a system of speed-firing involving two loaders passing him his Purdey hammer guns at full cock which enabled him on one occasion at Sandringham to kill 28 pheasants in one minute. Amazingly he was not apparently involved in any serious accidents, and when the Marquess died in 1923 aged 71, he did so suddenly from natural causes on the grouse moors, taking with him that day 51 grouse and a snipe.

# W. Wells

## Wine and spirit merchants

While some old-established family businesses in Ripon like Abbott's have survived, others, like Kearsley's and Smithson's have gone, and among these, regrettably, is William Wells and Sons, well known Wine and Spirit Merchants in the town over a number of generations, whose name can still be seen over their now long-closed shop in North Street.

Although they later claimed to have begun business in 1800, it is not clear on what that claim was based. Records show that the founder was William Wells, who hailed from Burneston near Bedale. He came to Ripon in 1840, then aged 16, and became a grocer's apprentice. In 1851 he married Anne Scott, daughter of an Old Market Place butcher, and in the same year took over the grocery business. Within a few years he could describe himself as a grocer, tea-dealer, seedsman and tallow chandler. His star was still rising, however, and in 1865 he diversified yet further to take over the premises of the wine and spirit business of William Morton in North Street. By 1875 Wells was advertising linseed cake and cigars as well as ale and porter, and by the 1890s award-winning ginger beer and aerated mineral waters also figured in their sales. It was around this time that the business was for some years confusingly given the address of 8 Old Market Place, before being redesignated again as North Street. Other branches were to open in Bedale and Thirsk.

William Wells was already involved in local politics, having joined Ripon Corporation in 1857, and in 1869-70 he held the city's top job as Mayor. Later a magistrate, he held a variety of other public offices, and was first chairman of the present Ripon Racecourse Company on the Boroughbridge Road site (1899). He eventually died in 1903, and control of the business then passed to his 45-year-old son Arthur, who was similarly active in local government and had been Mayor in 1898-99. Arthur also supported the Operatic Society and was a keen sportsman, his interests including athletics, rugby, golf, racing and cricket. President of the Ripon Cricket Club, his score of 152 on the Ripon ground was apparently a long-standing record, and he also became a Vice-President of the Yorkshire County Cricket Club.

Arthur's elder brother Thomas had similar interests and he too was active in public affairs, but was perhaps most warmly remembered for supplying a bottle of rum for the Workhouse plum pudding on Christmas Day. Thomas died in 1916 aged 62, while Arthur survived to the age of 77, dying in 1934.

The family business now moved on a generation to Arthur's sons, Norman and Wilfrid Wells. Norman had joined the army in 1914, aged 18, and although later invalided out, he went on to serve in the Second World War with the rank of Major. He was elected to Ripon Corporation after the war and became Mayor in 1956-7, maintaining a long established family tradition. For 25 years he was chairman of Ripon Racecourse Company and in 1962 was awarded the C.B.E. for political and public services. He lived until 1984, dying at the advanced age of 88.

The last member of the Wells family to be involved in the business was Wilfrid's son Scott Wells who ran it in partnership with Norman Wells' son-in-law Frank Haultain. Ill health, however, finally brought about the closure of the business in 1982.

# W. M. Abbott

## Cabinet manufacturer, upholsterer, and complete house furnisher

Long established family businesses are now a rarity in Ripon, but one that has successfully survived the passage of time is that of W. M. Abbott & Co., the household furnishing shop in North Street with the familiar long frontage.

16 Stock Rooms at North Street,
with Up-to-date Goods of dependable quality, at Moderate Prices.
Wood, Brass, Copper, and China Novelties, suitable for Wedding Presents, &c.
PIANOS & ORGANS.    Honest Value our Business Motto.
FACTORY—KIRKBY ROAD.

The advertisement in the picture dates to 1915 and sets out in some detail the range of goods then on offer, with both weddings and funerals catered for. Business was booming: the extensive premises included 16 stock rooms, and only a few years earlier a new furniture factory had been opened in Kirkby Road. The World War I Army Camp was to bring extra trade - "Officers' Field Kit and Camp Furniture" is highlighted in an otherwise very similar advert in 1918.

The then owner of the business, and the man whose enterprise had developed it, was William Middleton Abbott, born in 1856. Named William after his father, he gained Middleton from his mother's maiden name. Tradition has it that his father's business was founded in 1853 but, taken two years earlier, the 1851 census reveals that William Abbott (senior), then 38, was already a Journeyman Cabinet Maker; by 1861 he was a Master Cabinet Maker employing 2 men and 4 boys. Almost certainly his home and workshop was then near the *Black Bull* on the corner of Old Market Place and North Street.

By 1881, however, William had moved to No.11 Old Market Place (now part of the Kitchen and Bathroom Centre). His wife Elizabeth had died the year before, and William, then 68, was to die in December that year - but his occupation is now recorded as bookseller and stationer. This late change of career no doubt reflected the fact that by then he had passed on the cabinet-making business to his son, William Middleton Abbott, who is described in 1881 as a cabinet maker and upholsterer. He was then 25, his wife Ann was 27, and they had a new-born daughter Ada. They had taken over the family home and workshop across the Old Market Place next to the *Black Bull*.

However, he clearly had grand plans to expand the business, since within ten years it had moved to the present much larger premises in North Street, and in an advertisement of 1901 it could claim not only to have "extensive showrooms" but also to be "Patronised by Royalty". How that came about is unclear - who was the mysterious Royal sponsor?

In 1912 W. M. Abbott, now a company, opened a new furniture factory opposite the cemetery gates in Kirkby Road, and went on to build a fine reputation for making high quality reproduction furniture in the style of Chippendale, Sheraton and Hepplewhite. Clock cases were their speciality. However, times changed; in 1937 William Middleton Abbott died, aged 82, and the business was taken over by the sons of his second wife Ada. The Second World War was soon to have its effects, and in 1962 it was decided to close the factory and use only the workshop in North Street, but this too closed in the 1980s. The shop however continues, and in the new millennium the Abbott family still runs a successful house furnishing business there, responding to market forces and so keeping alive one of Ripon's longest established retail concerns.

# The Severs family

## Prominent in local business and the community

Many will recognise the dilapidated but still imposing structure in Spa Park that was once a drinking fountain. It is not of course in its original location - when first set up in 1875 it stood at the end of North Road, close to North Bridge, where the thirsty could refresh themselves as they reached or left the city outskirts. A few years later (1881) North Bridge was doubled in width in a more significant improvement to the area.

The drinking fountain was not just for people. The ground level trough (now filled in) held water for horses, cattle and other livestock, whilst the general public took their water from spring taps over the upper basin, guarded by grotesque animal heads. Around the top of the fountain ran the dedicatory inscription which

states that it was "erected for the use of the public by John Severs of Ripon, 1875", and the Mayor officially opened it on 7th September of that year. It was to survive at the roadside near North Bridge until 1929 when, regarded perhaps as an anachronism (or even obstacle?) in the new era of motor vehicles, it was moved to Spa Park.

Who was John Severs? Although in 1875 there was a 72-year-old carpenter and wheelwright of that name working in Bondgate Green, he is unlikely to have been able to afford the estimated cost of £130 which the project entailed. A much more likely candidate is the 38-year-old John Severs, married with a four-year-old daughter, who described himself a few years later in the 1881 census as a wool merchant.

He was probably the son of Thomas Severs, variously listed in trade directories from the 1840s onwards as a fellmonger, woolcomber and wool merchant, operating from premises in King St/Wellington St.

But there were more Severs in Ripon in those days as the other photograph reminds us. By 1881 No. 42 Market Place (now Row & Son) was occupied by another branch of the family, with another Thomas Severs, aged 38, and Charles J. Severs, aged 30 - formerly fellmongers, now goldsmiths - running a jewellery business there, and it is they no doubt who figure in the photograph which is

of this period. Sharing the house with her unmarried sons and unmarried daughter was Elizabeth Severs, aged 69.

Charles J. Severs went on to purchase No. 42 in 1894, but twenty-five years later in 1919 he sold it to W.D. Row, his former apprentice, who in fact seems to have been running the business since at least 1906. In 1932 it passed to his son Arthur Mallinson Row, and several generations later|his family still retain the business as A. M. Row and Son.

The office over Row's shop at 42 Market Place nowadays is the headquarters of the Ripon Local Studies Research Centre which has produced this book.

# The 1886 Festival

## A city festooned with flags and flowers

In an age of festivals, we are reminded that Ripon is no stranger to them - in fact the local tradition goes back well over 100 years to the great Millenary Festival of 1886. Although the Victorians are often thought of as a sombre and rather stuffy lot, there is no doubt that in Ripon they knew how to enjoy themselves, as the events of that first festival reveal.

Its origin lay in the fact that a lot of influential people in the town at that time, full of civic pride, wanted to win recognition for Ripon by holding a major event of national significance, and there happened to be a suitable hook to hang one on - an old tradition that Ripon had received a civic charter from King Alfred in 886, a thousand years earlier. The fact that this tradition sprang only from the writings of the eccentric 18thC antiquarian Thomas Gent, and that no trace of the charter could be found, acted as no deterrent, despite certain derisory comments from outside the town. It should be said in fairness however, that the Ripon of St.Wilfrid does of course date back to Anglo-Saxon times, and its ancient Horn may well be from that period - but an 886 Charter? No. King Alfred of Wessex had no interest or authority in these parts, and at that time was in any case fighting a war of survival against the Vikings.

Nevertheless, in 1886 the City Fathers went about preparing a festival in style, to be spread over a period of days. The inevitable Festival Committee did the planning, and a certain D'Arcy Ferris was placed in charge of the event as Master of the Revels. The Mayor was Alderman John Baynes, a slate merchant, and both the Dean (William Robert Freemantle) and the Bishop (William Boyd Carpenter) were actively involved since the opportunity was taken to include the 50th anniversary of the Diocese of Ripon in the Festival proceedings.

The opening day, Wednesday 25th August, began with a peal of the Cathedral bells lasting over three hours. Shops and public buildings, including the obelisk, were festooned with flags, bunting, flowers and evergreens, and entry to several streets, including Bondgate, was through large floral arches. The first major event was a grand civic procession of some 15 guest Mayors, from as

far away as Scarborough and Halifax, led by Mayor Baynes and the Sergeant-at-Mace. This entourage wound its way via Westgate, Trinity Lane and Coltsgate Hill back to the Square and then down Kirkgate to the Cathedral, where they were met by a cluster of clergy that included the Archbishop of York, who preached the sermon in the service that followed.

Afterwards the Mayor presided over a grand luncheon for the visiting dignitaries in the Victoria Hall (now Sigma Antiques), complete with toasts and speeches. Attention then switched to the Market Place, where (amidst more speeches) Dean Freemantle presented the Mayor with a Horn taken from the herd of Chillingham wild cattle. In the evening came the illuminations - an impressive torchlit procession through streets lit with Chinese and Japanese lanterns.

The climax of the Festival was undoubtedly a colourful historical pageant performed at Fountains Abbey on Friday 27th August and repeated the following day. A long procession of extraordinary floats wound its way from Studley Park to the abbey ruins, where an hour-long play about Robin Hood and Friar Tuck was performed before a large audience, many of whom had arrived by train. The festival ended the following Wednesday with a venison supper for all the performers. The weather had been good, and the organisers deemed the festival a brilliant success - in Ripon's history it was undoubtedly a week to remember.

# The 1896 and Later Festivals

## The festival idea catches on

So successful was the Millenary Festival of 1886 that many felt a similar event should be held every ten years, and when 1896 arrived, the decision was taken to go ahead with this. The fact that the Marquess of Ripon was to be Mayor that year may have been a consideration too, since he owned Fountains Abbey and Studley Park, and as in 1886 they were likely to play a major role in the festivities.

STREET OF OLD RIPON, ON THE ABBEY GREEN.
*(Drawn by Jas. Rogers).*

However there were also to be significant differences between the two events, and the plans for 1896 were arguably more ambitious. A huge stage set reconstructing an 'Old Ripon Street', complete with a gigantic model Obelisk, was to be built west of the abbey, and on the eastern side of the ruins a huge arena of 3500 seats would arise for viewing a grand pageant of English history. The libretto for this highlight event was written by Councillor Tom Williamson, an active thespian and prominent member of the paint and varnish family. He was to be Mayor the following year.

Guarantors of funding were found, and it was decided that should any profit be made, most should be given to local elementary schools. Once again a week late in August was the chosen time, again John Baynes

(though not now as Mayor) was put in overall charge, and again the Master of Revels was to be D'Arcy Ferris (though he now styled himself D'Arcy de Ferrars). Once more the bands played and the town was richly decorated with flags, drapes, lanterns and street arches.

The theme of the pageant was 'Boadicea to Victoria', and subjects were chosen from virtually every century between them, with much emphasis on well-known historical personages. The richly costumed performers processed from Studley Park to the abbey, to cavort in front of an appreciative audience. After the pageant came a performance of the Robin Hood/Friar Tuck play deemed to have been a hit in 1886 and so worth repeating (with much the same cast).

Another highlight of the 1896 Festival week was a public luncheon in the Victoria Hall at which the Mayoress (the Marchioness of Ripon) was presented with the extremely fine gold chain of office still worn by the Mayoress of today.

In the Cathedral a special service was held for the dedication of the East Window as a memorial to the late Dean Freemantle, who had died the year before, and there was an impressive torchlight procession through the town. On another day there was a cavalcade of decorated waggons and carriages out at Studley, and also a parade of bicycles - still a novelty. The week ended with a children's procession

DANE AND SAXON

133

illustrating nursery rhymes, and with maypole, morris and sword dancing - plus an ox-roast near the Ripon street stage-set. Interestingly, unlike 1886, a detailed photographic record was kept of the whole Festival.

By this time Ripon had developed a real taste for festivals, and after the Diamond Jubilee celebrations in 1897, the next opportunity came in 1904, the tercentenary of King James I's two charters of 1604. This festival was only a three-day affair, but included a Cathedral service, a luncheon, a play (not Robin Hood), music and dancing in the Spa Gardens, with fireworks to finish. Within two years (1906), it was festival time again: the twentieth anniversary of the Millenary Festival. Again a three-day event, it combined all the tried and tested ingredients apparently with great success, but it proved to be the last of the line - ten years on (1916) enthusiasm for a fun festival had been swamped by other feelings.

# Diamond Jubilee Celebrations in 1897

### Enhancing the City's appearance

When Ripon recently celebrated the most far-reaching refurbishment of the Market Place in its 800-year history, it was an informative experience to look back to another time when there were major changes taking place in the town centre, and people had to decide whether they were for or against them.

Although gas lamps had appeared around the edge of the Square in 1882, trees came later - in February 1897 in fact, when twelve lime trees were planted, ten by former Mayors of the City and two by the current Mayor and Mayoress. A good excuse, perhaps, for the inevitable post-planting civic luncheon at the *Unicorn*, but Edwardian postcards and interwar photographs show how far this soft landscaping undoubtedly enhanced the Market Place and proved the critics wrong. Even so the trees were beset with many hazards over the years to come, and it is to be hoped that their more recent replacements are very much of the hardy variety!

The photograph shows the Mayor of 1896/7, Tom Williamson, with the Dean and his civic colleagues, including his predecessor Lord Ripon and (far right) four-times mayor John Baynes, who had presided over the great

Millenary Festival of 1886.

Other changes were taking place in the Square in those days, quite apart from the appearance of trees around its perimeter. Perhaps with a view to removing unnecessary clutter, the four mini-obelisks which had long stood around the main Obelisk were removed in 1882, and in 1896 the

Crimean war cannon and the cast-iron drinking fountain suffered a similar fate. But there were arrivals as well as departures - in 1899 what were then regarded as lavishly-equipped underground public toilets were installed in the Square, amidst a plethora of jokes and protests (the toilets survived just long enough to achieve their centenary).

The surface of the Square has been an ongoing issue over the years, and it is interesting to note that John Aislabie had had it re-cobbled in 1702 at the time his Obelisk was being constructed. The presence of livestock at regular fairs and markets meant however that the surface was difficult to keep clean, and in 1900 the Corporation grasped the nettle and amidst the inevitable protests had the herring-bone patterned concrete paving laid that survived until 2000. Plus ça change.........

Back in 1897, there was more to celebrate than the tree-planting. It was after all Queen Victoria's Diamond Jubilee Year, and the Corporation decided that some permanent memorial must be created; a generous private donation made possible the construction of the Palace Road Clock Tower, inaugurated with a flourish the following year. But the Royal Jubilee was marked in other ways too - in June there were lavish street decorations (especially in Bondgate), special cathedral services, bonfires and fireworks, a free dinner for 300 over-60s, and medals and treats for the schoolchildren. It is interesting to compare all this with the Golden Jubilee celebrations of June 2002.

**Footnote:** the new trees in the Market Place look like maples but are Sweet Gums, originally from Mexico and eastern America, but known in this country since the 17thC. When they have settled in, they should produce gorgeous crimson colours in the autumn.

# Ripon's M.P.s

## Centuries of Parliamentary representation

Should it be required, evidence of Ripon's long history is afforded by the fact that it had representation in Parliament as long ago as 1295. Ripon first returned Members when Edward I sought the consent of the people for taxes that would help to pay for his war in Scotland. Ripon was then a borough belonging to the Archbishop of York, flourishing on its cloth industry and deemed important enough to be separately represented. It proved however to be something of a false start, since after 1337 Ripon provided no Members for over two hundred years, until the reign of Mary Tudor (1553).

From then until the late19thC Ripon had not one but two M.P.s, and they were usually recruited from the local landed gentry, for example Peter Yorke of Gouthwaite Hall in Nidderdale during Elizabeth's reign, and Sir William Mallorie of Studley Royal in early Stuart times. The latter represented Ripon in six parliaments between 1614 and 1640, and his son John Mallorie was Ripon's other representative in 1640. Two years later as a true Royalist he had the satisfaction of putting to flight a Roundhead force in the Market Place that had been vandalising the Minster. He was later to command the garrison of Skipton Castle during the greatest siege of the Civil War.

By the late 17thC significant political change was taking place. It had long been the custom for Ripon's M.P.s to be nominated by the Archbishop of York whose choice would then be rubber-stamped by the vote of the borough's burgage-holders, but by the 1670s there was a new spirit of independence in the town (to the annoyance of the Archbishop). John Aislabie, a Ripon M.P. from 1695 after succeeding the Mallories at Studley Royal, now helped to speed the decline of church control. In 1715, in a contested election, 169 burgesses voted and the Archbishop's candidate, his son, was defeated. Aislabie influence was now on the increase as four years later it was John Aislabie's son William who was elected, and he thereafter represented Ripon in every parliament until his death in 1781.

By the close of the 18thC Ripon as a parliamentary borough was very much in the pocket of the Studley Royal family, and Elizabeth Sophia Lawrence continued to buy up vote-bearing properties at every opportunity. One of the Studley family M.P.s was Frederick John Robinson who as Viscount Goderich was briefly Prime Minister in 1827. Whilst he was at No.10 the son was born who was later to become the Marquess of Ripon.

Once again, however, times and attitudes were changing. Under the Great Reform Act of 1832, the franchise was significantly widened to bring an end to 'pocket' boroughs. Contested elections became the norm and now it was the turn of the Studley influence to wane. Yet more change took place when the 1867 Reform Act reduced Ripon's representation to one M.P., and in 1885 the borough was merged in a much larger Ripon Division.

In 1910 the Hon. Edward Wood was elected to the Ripon constituency. He became a Minister in Baldwin's Conservative government of the mid-1920s, but then gave up his seat in 1926 to become Viceroy of India. Later he succeeded his father as Earl of Halifax and served as Foreign Secretary in the late 1930s. In 1940 he was seen by the peace party as a serious alternative to Churchill as Prime Minister. Since his time the Ripon seat (now covering Skipton too) has remained in Conservative hands except when Liberal David Austick captured it briefly in 1973.


# John Haddon Askwith

## Old Sleningford Hall and the Ripon connection

Old Sleningford Hall, in recent times the home of James and Juliet Ramsden, was built early in the 19thC by an enterprising young businessman whose roots embraced both the Ripon hostelries of the *Unicorn* and the *Royal Oak*. John

Haddon Askwith was born in 1782, the son of William Askwith, proprietor of the *Royal Oak* in Kirkgate and Mayor of Ripon in that year. As noted in a previous article, William Askwith had already earned the gratitude of the townsfolk several years earlier by arranging for fresh water from the millrace to be pumped up Duck Hill into the town for easier distribution. Years later, deafness and infirmity forced him to give up  the *Royal Oak* in his early sixties, and he died in 1814 aged 74.

Meanwhile his son John Haddon Askwith had enjoyed an unusual early career by becoming involved in the East Indies trade and allegedly returning from Mauritius with money after being a prisoner of the French during the Napoleonic War. Something of a speculator, he is also said to have owned lead mines in Wensleydale, and in 1810 bought from the Beckwith family the burnt ruins of Skirbeck Hall near Mickley which he rebuilt as the charming country house known since as Old Sleningford Hall.

This was to prove a busy period in Askwith's life. Some years earlier in 1774 his aunt Alice had married John Haddon, and in the same year Haddon inherited the *Unicorn* on the death of his mother Sarah. But only a few years later in 1780 Alice was left a widow, and it would seem that when her nephew John was born in 1782, he was named John Haddon Askwith in memory of his dead uncle. Thirty years later Aunt Alice died, and her favoured nephew inherited the *Unicorn*, no doubt living there for some time until Old Sleningford Hall was completed.

Records show that Askwith insured the *Unicorn* and its contents for £3000 in 1814, but it was soon time to move on. In 1817 he leased the *Unicorn* to Haseldine Sharpin of York, and in 1821 sold it to Elizabeth Sophia Lawrence of Studley Royal. By this time he would also have inherited some or all of the proceeds from the sale of his deceased father's *Royal Oak*.

In 1810 Askwith, aged 28, married Catherine Harrison, nine years his senior, and their first son arrived the following year, named William no doubt after his grandfather. In 1812 baby Catherine arrived, named after mother, followed by John Haddon junior in 1814. When Robert came along in 1815, significantly his place of birth was given as Sleningford, and this applied also to Thomas (1816) and Jane (1818).

But about this time Askwith pulled up his roots again, selling his recently built house to Thomas Staveley (see next article), who was to live there for the rest of his life. Where Askwith took his family is still unclear. When yet another child was born - Charlotte in 1823 - the birthplace given was Ripon, but Askwith's name is also linked to Norton Conyers Hall which in the early 19thC passed out of the ownership of the Graham family for several decades.

All that is known for certain is that Askwith's wife Catherine died early in 1824, aged 51, and he himself died four months later, aged only 42. They were buried at Pickhill, where their memorial - opposite those of three members of Catherine's family – is bathed on sunny days in the multi-coloured light from the church's west window. A tragically early end to lives which left nine young children to lament their loss.

# Thomas Kitchingman Staveley

## Sic transit gloria mundi

Thomas Kitchingman Staveley is a good local example of a man achieving his brief moment of glory and being remembered for it for the rest of his life. In Staveley's case it concerned his election as a liberal and reformist Member of Parliament for Ripon in the teeth of vigorous opposition from the entrenched and influential conservatives - who eventually proved too strong for him.

Born in 1791, he first appears on the scene as a Captain in the Royal Engineers during the Napoleonic War. In 1814, very near to the end of the war, he inherited the estate of General Miles Staveley of North Stainley Hall on the condition that he took the name and armorial bearings of the Staveleys, which he not surprisingly did (his original name was Hutchinson). Also in about 1818 he purchased Old Sleningford Hall from John Haddon Askwith who had recently rebuilt it after a fire, and Staveley lived there for the rest of his life.

Little more of him is then heard until 1832 which for the country as a whole was a year of great political excitement. The reason for this was the passing of the Great Reform Act and the general election that followed it. The Reform Act had a major impact on the Ripon scene, which previously had been a 'pocket borough' - in this case in the pocket of the Studley Royal family who owned the great majority of the burgage properties in the town, properties which carried the right

to vote. The 1832 Act abolished this ancient franchise and gave the right to vote to all householders rated at £10 or over, so creating about 320 voters.

This meant that Elizabeth Sophia Lawrence of Studley Royal would no longer be able to nominate Ripon's M.P.s, and for reformers in the town this was a great opportunity to reduce her influence. For the general election that was to follow, liberal reformist candidates were needed, if the Studley Royal Tory candidates were to be challenged, and at this juncture Thomas Staveley emerged from relative obscurity into the bright light of local politics. He and Colonel Crompton of Azerley Hall put themselves forward as the reformers' candidates and were returned, if by a very thin majority, amid scenes of riotous enthusiasm.

In those days, voting was an open and public affair, and in Ripon's case the hustings were in front of the Town Hall. The Orange (Reform) party entered the Market Place via Middle Street and the Blues via Westgate; the pubs were open, the ale flowed freely and there were numerous banners and bands playing music. The result known, a celebration banquet and ball had to be given at the expense of Staveley and Crompton, the victorious new M.P.s now acclaimed as heroes.

As a Member for Ripon, Staveley took a very active part in parliamentary affairs and pressed (in vain) for the adoption of vote by ballot. But soon another election was upon him - in 1835, and Staveley lost his seat, the main reason being the rigging of the vote by Studley Royal agents who arranged for many newly enfranchised 'householders' to be created on the Studley estate, in fields divided into plots with cow-houses as their homes. In 1835 not a single tenant of Mrs Lawrence voted for Staveley.

His moment of glory over, he was warmly praised by his supporters and presented with a silver plate before retiring to his Sleningford home. He served as a Magistrate for the Liberty of Ripon and as a Grammar School Governor, eventually dying in 1860. A stained glass window was put up in his memory in North Stainley church, which he had founded.

# Markenfield Hall

## A medieval gem

Markenfield Hall lies just outside Ripon, close to the medieval road south from the town, and is surrounded by its own farmland. It is a fortified manor house of moderate size, built in stone in the 14thC, set in a walled rectangular courtyard and surrounded by a protective moat. The battlements were perhaps intended more to impress others than to hold enemy forces at bay, but even so they may have been tested by the ravaging Scots during their incursions into the area after the English defeat at Bannockburn (1314).

We owe this manor house of the medieval gentry to

Canon John Markenfield, a lawyer and for a time Chancellor of the Exchequer, who obtained royal permission to crenellate, ie. fortify his house, in 1310 and after his death in 1323 further additions were made by his late medieval successors. Two of their tomb chests (1398 and 1497) can be seen in the north transept of Ripon Cathedral, the later monument bearing the effigy of Sir Thomas Markenfield, who was the Archbishop of York's High Steward in Ripon, and in 1485 High Sheriff of Yorkshire.

His son Sir Ninian Markenfield fought loyally for the king at Flodden in 1513 and died in 1528, but the fortunes of the family were soon to end in treason and disaster. In 1569 his grandson, Sir Thomas Markenfield, joined the Nortons of Norton Conyers and the Percys of Topcliffe in the Rising of the North, an attempt led by the earls of Northumberland and Westmorland to save the ancient Catholic faith in these parts. The rising however was crushed with little difficulty by the Queen's armies, Markenfield fled into exile abroad and his estates were confiscated.

Much of the house survives amazingly intact, and the moat provides an extremely attractive setting. Where would you find another unspoiled moated medieval manor house in the north of England?

Key rooms with Gothic window tracery include the Great Hall upstairs, the Solar or private chamber, and a Chapel - carefully restored in the 1980s - where monthly services are now held again. The chapel has an original spiral staircase ascending to the roof, with a striking turret. On the ground floor was the kitchen with other service and storage rooms. The Great Hall was originally approached by an external stone staircase, now long gone. Although there must have been a bridge across the moat from earliest times, the gatehouse is thought to have been rebuilt and perhaps re-sited in the 16thC, and the farm buildings are later.

Following the disaster of 1569 the estate passed to the Egerton family, Earls of Bridgewater, and then in 1761 was acquired by Fletcher Norton, first Lord Grantley of Markenfield, from whom it has passed to his heirs and successors. The property of absentee landlords and an appendage to larger estates, it served only as a working farm, but this sidelining has in fact helped to save the house from radical change and so preserve its medieval character. In recent years Markenfield Hall has benefited greatly from the loving care of Mr. Ian and Lady Deirdre Curteis, through whose efforts the ancient fireplace in the Great Hall is being reinstated to its original design.

# INDEX
## by David Lee